CW01281530

Social Control and Disorder in Football

This is the first book to focus on the interrelated issues of social control and disorder in football. It shows how the 'beautiful game' illuminates our understanding of the mechanisms and techniques of social control and regulation in contemporary societies.

It explores past, new, and continued responses from law enforcers, football associations, sport's governing bodies, the media, and international organizations to issues of disorder and misbehaviour in football, and how this is highly contested by fans and fan groups. Featuring the work of an international team of leading researchers in football and sport-related studies, the book examines key contemporary trends and topics including fan activism, football-specific legislation, power, violence, fan rivalries, subcultures, the policing of crowds, social sorting, and surveillance. Featuring diverse international cases, including the Qatar World Cup, stadium protests in Portland, Oregon, spectator violence in Polish football, social media and Brazilian football, and sectarianism in Scottish football, the book also looks ahead to what the future holds for the world's most popular sport.

This is an invaluable resource for students, researchers, or the general reader with an interest in the sociology of sport, criminology, sport management, and sports law.

Mark Turner is Senior Lecturer at Manchester Metropolitan University, UK, and the author of *The Safe Standing Movement in Football: Fan Networks, Tactics, and Mobilizations* published by Routledge in 2023. He is specifically interested in the application of relational sociology to the study of social networks, social movements, and activism, within different sport and leisure-based contexts. His work often cross pollinates ideas from sociology, political science, and cultural studies, to understand the impacts of events on the regulatory practices of those involved in the event planning and management of sport crowds and consumption.

Jan Andre Lee Ludvigsen is Senior Lecturer in International Relations and Politics with Sociology at Liverpool John Moores University, UK. His research focuses on the sociology and politics of sport, including security, surveillance, fan networks, and sport mega-events. He has authored four books, edited four special issues, and his work has appeared in journals such as *The British Journal of Sociology, Sociology Compass, Sociological Research Online, Journal of Consumer Culture*, and *International Review for the Sociology of Sport*.

Critical Research in Football
Series Editors:
Pete Millward, *Liverpool John Moores University, UK*
Jamie Cleland, *University of Southern Australia*
Dan Parnell, *University of Liverpool, UK*
Stacey Pope, *Durham University, UK*
Paul Widdop, *Manchester Metropolitan University, UK*

The *Critical Research in Football* book series was launched in 2017 to showcase the inter- and multi-disciplinary breadth of debate relating to 'football'. The series defines 'football' as broader than association football, with research on rugby, Gaelic and gridiron codes also featured. Including monographs, edited collections, short books and textbooks, books in the series are written and/or edited by leading experts in the field whilst consciously also affording space to emerging voices in the area, and are designed to appeal to students, postgraduate students and scholars who are interested in the range of disciplines in which critical research in football connects. The series is published in association with the *Football Collective*, @FB_Collective.

Available in this series:

LGBT Football Fans
Authenticity, Belonging and Visibility
Rory Magrath

Football and Diaspora
Connecting Dispersed Communities through the Global Game
Edited by Jeffrey W. Kassing and Sangmi Lee

Football, Power, and Politics in Argentina
Eugenio Paradiso

Women's Football, Culture, and Identity
Kate Themen

Social Control and Disorder in Football
Responses, Regulation, Rupture
Edited by Mark Turner and Jan Andre Lee Ludvigsen

https://www.routledge.com/Critical-Research-in-Football/book-series/CFSFC

Social Control and Disorder in Football
Responses, Regulation, Rupture

Edited by
Mark Turner and Jan Andre Lee Ludvigsen

LONDON AND NEW YORK

First published 2024
by Routledge
4 Park Square, Milton Park, Abingdon, Oxon OX14 4RN

and by Routledge
605 Third Avenue, New York, NY 10158

Routledge is an imprint of the Taylor & Francis Group, an informa business

© 2024 selection and editorial matter, Mark Turner and Jan Andre Lee Ludvigsen; individual chapters, the contributors

The right of Mark Turner and Jan Andre Lee Ludvigsen to be identified as the authors of the editorial material, and of the authors for their individual chapters, has been asserted in accordance with sections 77 and 78 of the Copyright, Designs and Patents Act 1988.

All rights reserved. No part of this book may be reprinted or reproduced or utilised in any form or by any electronic, mechanical, or other means, now known or hereafter invented, including photocopying and recording, or in any information storage or retrieval system, without permission in writing from the publishers.

Trademark notice: Product or corporate names may be trademarks or registered trademarks, and are used only for identification and explanation without intent to infringe.

British Library Cataloguing-in-Publication Data
A catalogue record for this book is available from the British Library

Library of Congress Cataloging-in-Publication Data
Names: Turner, Mark (Sport sociologist), editor. | Ludvigsen, Jan Andre Lee, editor.
Title: Social control and disorder in football : responses, regulation, rupture / edited by Mark Turner and Jan Andre Lee Ludvigsen.
Description: Abingdon, Oxon ; New York, NY : Routledge, 2024. | Series: Critical research in football | Includes bibliographical references and index.
Identifiers: LCCN 2023055394 | ISBN 9781032591223 (hardback) | ISBN 9781032591230 (paperback) | ISBN 9781003453062 (ebook)
Subjects: LCSH: Soccer fans. | Spectator control. | Social control. | Stadiums—Security measures. | Hosting of sporting events—Security measures. | Soccer hooliganism—Prevention. | Soccer fans—Law and legislation.
Classification: LCC GV943.9.F35 S627 2024 | DDC 796.334—dc23/eng/20231220
LC record available at https://lccn.loc.gov/2023055394

ISBN: 978-1-032-59122-3 (hbk)
ISBN: 978-1-032-59123-0 (pbk)
ISBN: 978-1-003-45306-2 (ebk)

DOI: 10.4324/9781003453062

Typeset in Optima
by codeMantra

Contributors

Mateusz Dróżdż is Attorney-at-law and owner of a law firm. He is Lecturer at Lazarski University, Poland, and Arbitrator at the Football Arbitration Court in Polish Football Association. In 2020–2021, he was Chairman of the supervisory board of Górnik Polkowice, in 2021–2023 he was President of Widzew Łódź, and in 2021–2022 he was Member of the Audit Committee of the First Football League.

Chris W. Henderson is Assistant Teaching Professor at the University of Rhode Island, USA. His research focuses on how people with limited access to institutional power utilize the affective bonds of sport fandom to form communities of care while enacting change in sports organizations. Chris teaches classes on sport history, sport and gender, sport and race, and sport media.

Radosław Kossakowski is Professor in Sociology at University of Gdańsk, Poland. His research fields are the sociology of sport, football studies, qualitative research, and masculinities studies. He has published his articles, among others, in *Sport in Society*, *Sociology of Sport Journal*, *International Review for the Sociology of Sport*, *East European Politics and Societies*, and *Soccer & Society*.

Pratik Nyaupane is a PhD student at the Annenberg School for Communication at the University of Southern California, USA, where he explores the intersection between culture, technology, and policing. As a doctoral researcher, Nyaupane has been exploring the ways in which technology is used as a form of state and private power. His most recent projects consist of evaluating policing and surveillance technologies on university campuses, sports stadiums, and national citizenship registries.

Renan Petersen-Wagner is Senior Lecturer in Sport Business and Marketing at Leeds Beckett University, UK. His research interests span media and social theories, with particular focus on the platformization of the sport and media nexus. He co-authored *The UEFA European Football Championships: Politics, Media Spectacle and Social Change* (Routledge, 2022), and his research has appeared in diverse journals such as *Convergence: The* *international Journal of Research into New Media Technologies*, *International Review for the Sociology of Sport*, *Leisure Studies*, *Journal of Sport & Social Issues*, *Current Sociology*, and *Sport in Society*.

Joel Rookwood is Lecturer and Course Director for the Sport and Exercise Management degree at University College Dublin, Ireland. He is also a visiting fellow in Sport Marketing and Management at the University of Vic – Central Catalunya, Spain. Joel has worked at 21 football mega-events in various capacities and his research examines football fandom, events, governance, and international development.

Christie Scanlon is an academic at UCFB Etihad Campus in Manchester, UK, specializing in the study of social sciences in sport. He is also a PhD researcher in Sociology at Liverpool John Moores University, UK, and has held a number of positions in the football industry. Christie also runs a podcast dedicated to exploring the intersections of sport and social science and has been featured in a number of professional publications.

Ian Woolsey is Senior Lecturer in Sociology at Sheffield Hallam University, UK.

Acknowledgements

As the editors, we wish to begin by thanking Simon Whitmore and Rebecca Connor from Routledge for their outstanding guidance and support throughout this and other projects that we have been fortunate enough to work with them on. We also thank Peter Millward for all his support throughout the years.

Naturally, given that this book is – and must be understood and read as – a collective effort, we are indebted to, and thank each author for their valuable contributions to this edited collection. From the point where we first reached out to potential authors with our idea in the final months of 2022, until we submitted the complete manuscript, roughly a year later, we have been privileged enough to collaborate with an exceptionally enthusiastic group of scholars who produce important and pioneering work. We had the pleasure of putting together this work into this volume.

Finally, Mark wants to thank his wife Kate and two children Isaac and Jonah for their invaluable support during the past few years throughout which much of this material was conceived, coordinated, worked, and written up. Jan extends his thanks to colleagues in Liverpool John Moores University's departments of International Relations and Politics and Sociology. He is also grateful for chats, discussions, and collaborations with David Webber, John Hayton, Renan-Petersen-Wagner, Jack Sugden, Paul Anderson, and Seamus Byrne. He would like to thank Mark, for this and also their other collaborative efforts and projects. Finally, Jan thanks his family for all their support.

1 Introduction

Social (Dis)Order and Control

Mark Turner and Jan Andre Lee Ludvigsen

Introduction

This book represents a collective effort to further advance and open new debates on *social control* and *disorder* in the world's most popular sport: association football (soccer). And so, it is one of the first texts that explicitly address the two key concepts here – social control and social disorder – as applied directly to various football-related topics including security and safety, policing, legislation, the control of football spaces and football fan cultures, identities, and practices. At the time of writing, it is clear that – over the last ten years – a number of key developments have taken place in diverse global football contexts. These developments, individually and collectively highlight the relevance of the visible and invisible efforts to ensure that football is '*secured*', '*controlled*', and '*ordered*'. Despite this, there are of course times where football matches (domestically and internationally) have become sites of *disorder* in recent years. This complex relationship between control and disorder, thus, remains omnipresent, and a contested terrain, in twenty-first-century football. This book attempts to gauge the various cultural and spatial consequences and social costs of social control and disorder in football and also unpack their wider sociological and political significance.

Concerning recent events, perhaps most notably, this involves the large-scale disorder that took place outside Wembley, London, on the day of the Euro 2020 final (played in 2021) between Italy and England (Lee Ludvigsen, 2022a). Then, in the subsequent 2021/2022 season, English football saw the rise in reported anti-social behaviour and pitch-invasions when stadiums reopened after Covid-19 closed stadiums throughout 2020 and 2021 (Pearson and Stott, 2022). In other contexts, too, throughout 2022, critical questions of safety and security in football were also asked following the tragic Youande Stadium disaster in Cameroon, in January 2022, where eight people died in a crush during a Africa Cup of Nations match (The Guardian, 2022) and then the 2022 Champions League final at *Stade de France* which was described as a 'near-miss' in the Independent Panel Review report following the mismanagement of crowds and other events surrounding the *Stade de France* final between Liverpool and Real Madrid in May 2022.[1] And most recently

DOI: 10.4324/9781003453062-1

at the UEFA 2023 Champions League final in Istanbul, reports emerged that Manchester City supporters were unable to return to their city centre hotels until past 3am after a scramble for shuttle buses at the end of the game, with some left stranded for more than an hour and a half before they could make the 15 mile journey back to the city centre (Boffey, 2023).

However, while images, reports, and headlines about social and public *disorder* in football are, arguably, most commonplace historically and presently, we would argue that it is also crucial to understand how various social control mechanisms are in place in football in order to make football more *'orderly'*, more *'regulated'* but simultaneously, and often, more commercially viable and lucrative. Historically, these social control responses, including new legislation, international treaties, and policing methods, have often followed key moments or tragedies in the sport including, for example, the tragedies of Heysel, the Bradford City stadium fire, and Hillsborough (Pearson and Stott, 2022; Turner, 2023). And it could reasonably be argued that, at the time of writing, we again find ourselves at such a critical juncture in football *vis-à-vis* safety, security, sustainability, and governance (see Turner and Lee Ludvigsen, 2023a, 2023b; Turner, 2023). At this critical juncture, questions regarding safety and security – and, indeed, how this should be ensured – should be a key priority for policymakers, football authorities, and academics alike. Here, a new regulatory regime is being prefigured to respond to new ruptures and critical junctures on crowd management, policing, and supporter engagement.

Hence, the backdrop and events described above feed into one of the starting points for this edited collection – namely, that the concepts of social control and social disorder are tightly attached to elite football across various continents in the twenty-first century. As such, at this crucial point in time, we argue it is imperative to reconsider them from social scientific perspectives. This represents the core contribution of this edited collection, with chapters drawing from various academic traditions and disciplines including, *inter alia*, sociology, criminology, cultural studies, social movement studies, and digital sociology.

The Aims of This Collection

It is clear that the cultures, issues, and mechanisms of, or related to, social control and disorder have long existed in the social world of sport. The topic of 'disorder' – in football's context – has historically been devoted much academic attention, and often in the contexts of so-called 'football hooliganism', football-related disorder (e.g., O'Neill, 2005; Marsh et al., 1980), 'risk fans' (Pearson and Stott, 2022; Lee Ludvigsen, 2022b) or 'ultras' (Testa, 2018). Moreover, beyond this, other scholars, including Groombridge (2017), Blackshaw and Crabbe (2004), Atkinson and Young (2008), Millward et al. (2022), and Tsoukala (2009) have all documented how we should seriously yet critically approach sport as a site wherein social control mechanisms are implemented, tested, and extended from. In football, *dispositifs* or apparatuses of social control that exercise power – to use some of Foucault's (2008) grammar – may be seen in a number of ways across various global football contexts and – crucially for this collection – they span a number of authorities and 'social control agents' (Tsoukala, 2009) within and outside the sport across various continents including, but not limited to security agencies, governments, football associations, clubs, private security companies, and firms. Together, these constitute a security and safety field or arena in professional football (Turner and Lee Ludvigsen, 2023b). As Tsoukala (2009) demonstrates, the agents of this field often possess the *definitional power* to set out how disorder should be controlled. Focusing on the pan-European context after 1985, she writes:

> Social control [in football] became increasingly anticipatory, with assessment of the potential dangerousness of football supporters left to the discretion of public and private security agents, who were free to set and amend the criteria used to subject individuals to an ever-growing control apparatus. (p. 58)

Yet, as some of this collection's chapters will reveal (Chapters 5, 7, and 8), this increasingly anticipatory stance can be located outside the European context, too. In practice, this has meant that the *key spaces* of football – the stadiums and their surrounding spaces – are typically equipped with state-of-the-art surveillance technologies (Klauser, 2017; Turner and Lee Ludvigsen, 2023). Moreover, football events and crowds are subject to highly specialized and costly policing operations (Pearson and Stott, 2022; O'Neill, 2005). In addition, there are also a number of 'football-specific' laws, regulations, and recommendations that exist on both on national (Pearson and Stott, 2022) and continent-wide levels (e.g., the Council of Europe Conventions from 1985 and 2016 relating to safety and security in football; see Byrne and Lee Ludvigsen, 2023). As other scholars have displayed, it is also not uncommon that exceptional measures are implemented in football (and target fans) and arrive with serious implications on fans' civil liberties or human rights (for wider discussions on this, see Pearson, 1999; Testa, 2018).

However, all this is often justified, as Pearson (1999) argues, on the basis that football fans are constructed as 'legitimate targets' for draconian and exceptional social control mechanisms and legislation. Indeed, many of Pearson's concerns from over twenty years ago may be echoed at the time of writing this chapter and editing this collection. Pearson writes:

> social control sanctions upon all football fans have become *more* stringent and restrictive on civil liberties, with an increasing amount of legislative power available to deal with 'hooligans', and a growth in extra-legal and 'undercover' policing powers and tactics. In effect […] those who attend football matches are still seen as legitimate targets for,

rather than victims of, over-the-top policing, crowd violence, and any tragedy which might befall them.

This is important because it is not merely the recent incidents of social disorder in the football world mentioned above that this book uses as a starting point. In fact, the medley of social control techniques that have been used, or are still in use, in football can be historically traced, and thus are temporally sensitive. Indeed, this suggests that football fans across many national contexts are still considered 'legitimate targets' for innovative, restrictive policies, technologies, and legislation.

By appreciating the contemporary but also the historical significance of social control and disorder in football, this book seeks to continue the academic tradition – and the growing tradition of this book series – of utilizing football to examine the wider socio-political trends. Indeed, this edited collection pays attention to how the various institutions involved, in some way, in football – for example, clubs, authorities, football authorities, the police, or international organizations – attempt to respond to, and regulate, both prospects and realities of social disorder and insecurity, and thereby aim to ensure that football's spaces remain controlled in the most popular football leagues and events in the world.

However, most attempts to control, secure, or govern football fans, spaces, and cultures have important social costs (Spaaij, 2013; Tsoukala, 2008), and are often the site of supporter-led contestations. And, as this book is concerned with, this raises important questions of how different types of football fans as a non-uniform social group are situated within the wider discourses of disorder and control and, indeed, how they contest and react to this, as important *stakeholders* of the modern game (see Cleland et al., 2018). Indeed, as our own single and co-authored scholarship shows, issues around security, safety, and social control in football have led to supporter mobilizations that may be traced back to key, transformative events in the 1980s, including the Heysel and Hillsborough tragedies, but also the consumer-oriented drive leading to an enhanced emphasis on control and regulation across football stadiums around the world (see Turner, 2023; Turner and Lee Ludvigsen, 2023a, 2023b; Lee Ludvigsen, 2022a). Ultimately, social control and disorder in football remain contested domains.

***

The subtitle of this book is '*responses, regulation, rupture*'. Importantly, this speaks to the overarching purpose of this book. We are concerned here with how the safety and security imperatives in football are responded to how they are regulated; and how, occasionally, internal or external societal ruptures have wide-ranging consequences for different fan cultures and communities. Thus, the various chapters of this edited collection are bound together by the different authors' motivations to examine critically the myriad of current issues, responses, and policies related to the mechanisms of social control and notions or problems of disorder in contemporary global football.

Because football remains such a fruitful and proven site for the understanding of 'the expansion of wider social control agendas' in sporting and leisure spheres (Giulianotti and Klauser, 2011: 8) that, importantly, intersect with urban and public spaces, this book will examine how important issues of safety and security in football are responded to across various national, social, and legal contexts including European, Western Asian, South American, and North American football.

Significantly, it will examine how various types of 'disorder', both in 'offline' and 'online' settings, are responded to by authorities within sport and beyond. In order to achieve these aims, the edited collection has primarily three objectives and, concurrently, academic debates that it seeks to advance further. The three objectives are:

- To explore the new and continued responses to 'disorder' and 'misbehaviour' in football from law enforcers, football associations and/or authorities, policy-makers, and clubs;
- To shed a light on football fans as *responsive* actors – and stakeholders – that *impact* and are *impacted* by social control apparatuses in football.
- To launch a cross-disciplinary research agenda for future work on social control and disorder in sport, and ensure that this research agenda is compatible with wider but related projects on sport and crime (Atkinson and Young, 2008; Groombridge, 2017; Millward et al., 2022), sport and policing (Pearson and Stott, 2022), and sport, security, and safety (Turner, 2023; Turner and Lee Ludvigsen, 2023a; Lee Ludvigsen, 2022a).

It is hoped that, by working towards these three inter-related objectives, this edited collection will make an important social scientific contribution by providing a range of analyses that capture the intersections between fan cultures, football governance, social control, all of which – beyond academic spheres – constitute highly relevant topics for policy-makers, clubs, football associations and the wider 'football industry' in the twenty-first century.

Chapter Overview

In this section, we provide a brief description of the individual chapters of this book. This edited collection consists of nine chapters, which we briefly summarize here. Next up, in Chapter 2, Radosław Kossakowski and Mateusz Dróżdż zooms in on the Polish context. Specifically, they are critically approaching the ways in which sport events and football, in particular, have been subjected to a raft of legal tools from the late 1980s until the present day. In doing so, they make the case for a separate law on the safety and organization of football games and highlight how some fans have attempted to resist legal and social control mechanisms. In Chapter 3, we are introduced by Ian Woolsey to the contested spaces of English football. Drawing upon the work of Zygmunt Bauman, Woolsey explores the social spacing of football by drawing upon fieldwork with Sheffield Wednesday supporters. In particular, Woolsey shows how a set of 'traditional' supporters seek to manage what they perceive as 'their' spaces and protect these from 'modern football'. The social control of football spaces is also a key theme in Chapter 4. Here, Joel Rookwood draws upon ethnographic fieldwork at the 2011 Asian Cup, the 2019 FIFA Club World Cup and, most recently, the 2022 World Cup in – all hosted in Qatar – to explore how international football fans perceived the social control mechanisms enacted for the 22nd men's World Cup in November and December 2022. Overall, Rookwood's empirical account highlights not only the unique security-related challenges in Qatar, but also reflects on which lessons that may be learned concerning crowd management and security in football.

Then, in Chapter 5, Renan Petersen-Wagner looks at how the sale of alcohol in Brazilian football stadiums which, historically, has been controlled was framed in media discourses before the 2014 World Cup in Brazil. His analysis therefore shows the interactions between football authorities' demands and local contexts and how the regulation of alcohol in the Brazilian context was impacted by these state and non-state interactions. Petersen-Wagner's chapter thus sheds a light on the *local-global* negotiations that take place in the attempts to control football spaces. In Chapter 6, Christie Scanlon focuses on Scottish football cultures. Specifically, Scanlon examines 'sectarianism' in the case of Scottish fan culture and society and the ways in which this has been responded to, criminalized and how it, in light of wider social changes, has attained a digital element through online and social media abuse that allow sectarian messages to be disseminated online.

In Chapter 7, Chris Henderson and Pratik Nyaupane examine how in US professional soccer, organized fan groups practise a subculture that sustains the lives of marginalized people within the group and provides a platform for resistant politics. Soccer leagues and teams engage with these fan groups in order to materially and ideologically prevent potential disruption of their spaces and brands through a practice they conceptualize as 'cultural extraction'. The purpose of cultural extraction is to at once depoliticize subculture and capitalize on it by claiming some elements as belonging to the institution and policing others. The soccer companies incorporate organized fandom into inclusionary branding reducing subcultural practices with distinct collective politics to identity-based spectacle in support of the broader cause of consumer-based team support. The chapter thus demonstrates how cultural extraction limits US professional soccer leagues' efforts to become more tolerant and diverse places by evaluating the public contestations over fan-generated subculture in Portland, Oregon, and Los Angeles.

In the final chapter, Chapter 8, we (Turner and Lee Ludvigsen) examine how supporters resist and, in some cases, campaign against social control mechanisms in football. While we seek to expand on our earlier, mobilized concept of the 'fan-opticon' here (Turner and Lee Ludvigsen, 2023a), we also show evidence of a culture of resistance that exist in some European football contexts and which is historically traceable as several of the chapters in this book showcases, too.

Note

1 See: https://www.nytimes.com/2023/02/13/sports/soccer/champions-league-final-report-liverpool-fans.html.

References

Atkinson, M & Young, K (2008) *Deviance and Social Control in Sports*. Champaign, IL. Human Kinetics.

Blackshaw, T & Crabbe, T (2004) *New Perspectives on Sport and 'Deviance': Consumption, Performativity and Social Control*. London. Routledge.

Boffey, D (2023) Uefa treated us like cattle at Istanbul Champions League final, say supporters. *The Guardian*. Available from: https://www.theguardian.com/football/2023/jun/11/uefa-treated-fans-at-istanbul-champions-league-final-like-cattle-say-supporters.

Byrne, S & Lee Ludvigsen, J A (2023) The duty of engagement: An analysis of the 2016 European Convention on an Integrated Safety, Security and Service Approach at Football Matches and Other Events. *Entertainment and Sports Law Journal* 21(1), 1–12.

Cleland, J, Doidge, M, Millward, P & Widdop, P (2018) *Collective Action and Football Fandom: A Relational Sociological Approach*. Cham. Springer.

Foucault, M (2008) *Security, Territory, Population: Lectures at the Collège de France, 1977–78*. Basingstoke. Palgrave.

Giulianotti, R & Klauser, F (2011) Introduction: Security and surveillance at sport mega events. *Urban Studies* 48(15), 3157–3168.

Groombridge, N (2017) *Sports Criminology: A Critical Criminology of Sports and Games*. Bristol. Policy Press.

Klauser, F (2017) *Surveillance and Space*. London. Sage.

Lee Ludvigsen, J A (2022a) *Sport Mega-Events, Security and Covid-19: Securing the Football World*. London. Routledge.

Lee Ludvigsen, J A (2022b) *Football and Risk: Trends and Perspectives*. London. Routledge.

Marsh, P, Rosser, E & Harré, R (1980) *The Rules of Disorder*. London. Routledge.

Millward, P, Lee Ludvigsen, J A & Sly, J (2022) *Sport and Crime: Towards a Critical Criminology of Sport*. London. Routledge.

O'Neill, M (2005) *Policing Football: Social Interaction and Negotiated Disorder*. Basingstoke. Palgrave.

Pearson, G (1999) Legitimate targets? The civil liberties of football fans. *Journal of Civil Liberties* 4(1), 28–47.

Pearson, G & Stott, C (2022) *A New Agenda for Football Crowd Management: Reforming Legal and Policing Responses to Risk*. Cham. Palgrave Macmillan.

Spaaij, R (2013) Risk, security and technology: Governing football supporters in the twenty-first century. *Sport in Society* 16(2), 167–183.

Testa, A (2018) The all-seeing eye of state surveillance in the Italian football (soccer) terraces: The case study of the football fan card. *Surveillance and Society* 16(1), 69–83.

The Guardian (2022) 'Why did people have to die?': Cameroon mourns after stadium tragedy'. *The Guardian*. Available from: https://www.theguardian.com/football/2022/jan/25/why-did-people-have-to-die-cameroon-mourns-after-stadium-tragedy.

Tsoukala, A (2008) Football supporters' rights: A lost cause? *The International Sports Law Journal* 3–4, 89–92.

Tsoukala, A (2009) *Football Hooliganism in Europe: Security and Civil Liberties in the Balance*. Basingstoke. Palgrave.

Turner, M (2023) *The Safe Standing Movement in Football: Fan Networks, Tactics, and Mobilisations*. London. Routledge.

Turner, M & Lee Ludvigsen, J A (2023a) Theorizing surveillance and social spacing through football: The fan-opticon and beyond. *Sociology Compass* 17(2), 1–14.

Turner, M & Lee Ludvigsen, J A (2023b) Safety and security Battles: Unpacking the players and arenas of the safe standing movement in English football (1989–2022). *Sociological Research Online*, online first, 1–18.

2 The Evolution of Legal Tools Dedicated to Sport Mass Events in Poland and its Socio-Cultural Consequences

The Law Against Supporters?

Radosław Kossakowski and Mateusz Dróżdż

Introduction

The topic related to the relationship between fan behaviour and legal tools for controlling such behaviour has been undertaken in numerous scholarly works. This is primarily associated with intense legislative changes dedicated to football matches and fans, which are implemented in various countries (see Dróżdż, 2014; Giulianotti, 2011; Hopkins and Treadwell, 2014). However, the analysis of legislative transformations in football and fan behaviour cannot be detached from the broader socio-cultural context. The introduction of legal amendments remains, in many countries, in line with broader trends of a moral and civilizational nature. These include strategies of state authorities aimed at 'civilizing' fan behaviours (Flint and Powell, 2014: 71). For example, Richard Giulianotti (1994) traces the implementation of new laws in the United Kingdom concerning football matches and observes that such regulations come a consequence of the fact that authorities have defined football violence as a 'social problem'. The law also addresses such phenomena as 'extensive joyfulness' among football spectators (Carlsson and Backman, 2023). Growing social sensitivity means that behaviour that was until recently accepted in the social space is today becoming an object of infamy and is being criminalized (Waiton, 2014). Fan communities are still treated as a 'social problem', the only difference being that legal and institutional restrictions are no longer explained by the need to tackle the 'hooligan disease'. The authorities of some countries very often try to prevent any possible undesirable acts around football matches, but as a result, the level of control and restrictions aimed at football means restricting the fundamental rights of freedom of people who just want to watch the game.

Many studies also mention the role of the commercialization of football in the tightening of laws regarding fan behaviour. Transforming football into a commercially driven product goes hand in hand with the attempt to exchange 'rebellious' and unpredictable fans (sometimes prone to aggressive behaviour) for fan-consumers. These fan-consumers support the football team and fit into clubs' business models as enterprises (Antonowicz et al., 2015; Crabbe and Brown 2004). It's worth noting that changes in law are somewhat parallel to the processes of commercialization. For example, in England, changes in the law (as well as stadium infrastructure) regarding football matches were a consequence of events like the Hillsborough stadium disaster in 1989, when 89 people died due to the disastrous organization of the event. The formation of the professional football league Premier League in 1992, which revolutionized the commercial significance of football, only reinforced the processes initiated by legal changes (e.g., the requirement to introduce seated areas in stadiums, see Turner, 2022).

The main aim of the following chapter is to describe and analyse the changes in the law dedicated to fan behaviour in Poland, together with an analysis of the broader socio-political context in which these changes were introduced and the reactions of fans to these changes. The article fills a gap in the literature on the issue in question due to its interdisciplinary (legal-sociological) nature. It can also serve as a comparative case study for researchers from other countries.

The Law Dedicated to Football Matches in Poland

Tracing the evolution of legal changes dedicated to football and fans in Poland is not an easy task. This is related not only to the turbulent history of the Polish state in recent decades (including the systemic transformation in 1989 and the transition from communism to free-market capitalism) but also to the fact that fan behaviour has become a political issue in recent times. Therefore, we focus our analysis on the situation that occurred after the 1989 transformation, considering that the issues related to sports events had also been of legislative interest in earlier periods (Dróżdż, 2020). It is worth emphasizing that the introduction of regulations into the Polish legal system regarding the organization and safety of mass events did not result from a thorough analysis of sports law or sports development. The latest Law on the Safety of Mass Events, which regulates issues related to artistic and entertainment events as well as sports events, including football matches, was introduced solely due to the growing problem of stadium hooliganism and the organization of the UEFA European Football Championship in 2012. The first Law on the Safety of Mass Events from 1997 was not motivated by a desire to regulate the commercialization or professionalization of sports (or the issue of stadium hooliganism, which had an unprecedented character in the 1990s; see Kossakowski, 2021). Its enactment was primarily driven by a tragic event on November 24, 1994, during a rock concert at an entertainment hall in Gdańsk (where seven people died due to a fire). Therefore, the legislative actions had a purely preventive nature.

Until 1997, the Polish legal system did not have an act or any other legislative documents that comprehensively regulated the issues related to mass events, including sports ones. Given that the commercialization of mass events was already a widespread phenomenon in Europe, and cases of hooliganism were observed in Polish stadiums[1], the legislative inaction in this regard was incomprehensible and should not have occurred. It could be argued that the lack of regulations on this matter was a direct cause of the development of stadium hooliganism in Poland. The evolution of sports events, or rather a kind of phenomenon associated with these events, was already so complexly developed by the end of the twentieth century that an act regulating mass events, including sports events, should have been enacted by the legislature much earlier, especially since Poland had previously ratified the European Convention on spectator violence and misbehaviour at sports events, particularly football matches (drawn up on August 19, 1985), which Poland only ratified in 1995. The absence of regulations in this area also led to divergent interpretations regarding the tort and contractual liability of sports event organizers.

Despite the enactment of laws and other acts related to the organization of mass events, there is a complete lack of recognition of the scale of transformations to which sports, and thus sports events, are subject. In this case, the legislator often introduces regulations too late, and as was the case in Poland, it also creates norms that cannot be effective due to their lack of alignment with social realities. Furthermore, in principle, these regulations do not lead to the commercial development of sports events – mass events because they have a very restrictive effect. For example, to offer stronger alcohol (legally, only beer up to 3.5% is allowed – only during matches that are not classified as high-risk matches) in the so-called 'skybox' lounges intended for VIP guests, the organizer of the sports event must 'exclude' such places from the sports event. As a result, there are sectors subject to the law and those that are excluded from it in the same stadium.

Today, it is also clear that the legislator, in pursuit of the goal of combating stadium hooliganism, introduced provisions that do not guarantee the individual's constitutionally protected rights and freedoms. The provisions of this law were subject to constitutional review by the Constitutional Tribunal on three occasions (once the proceedings were terminated for formal reasons, the second provision allowing for criminal sanctions for violating the regulations of the mass event organizer was found unconstitutional, and in the most recent case, the Tribunal declared the constitutionality of the so-called club ban – imposed by the organizer, although, in the justification, the Tribunal indicated that the application by the Commissioner for Civil Rights should be formulated differently).

The Law on the Safety of Mass Events was implemented in the Polish legal system in 1997. The innovative content of the document aimed to solve the problems related to the occurrence of dangerous situations during mass events. Unfortunately, the assumptions deviated from reality. Certain legislative shortcomings were immediately 'exploited' by organizers of large events, and they bypassed the obligation to carry out all activities related, for example, to obtaining permission for a mass event. After approximately 20 years of the law's implementation, a new version of it was enacted, but in reality, it did not lead to an improvement in the provisions. Its primary objective was to combat the so-called stadium hooliganism closely related to football.

The law's focus on essentially one phenomenon (related to football) means that organizers of other mass events had difficulty applying it. Unfortunately, the enactment of the Law on the Safety of Mass Events, or its amendments, took place with significant involvement from the press, radio, and television, which led to haste in its adoption, which is not advisable in the creation of legislation. Furthermore, this situation indirectly encourages a specific trend, which involves the systematic expansion of the scope of criminalization of certain behaviours occurring at the location and during the duration of a mass event, even though the main problem related to stadium hooliganism has been occurring outside of these events for many years. It has been evident for quite some time that Polish football hooligans have been moving their activities away from the stadiums. Restrictive laws and the presence of surveillance cameras in stadiums have reduced acts of aggression within the stadiums, while fan confrontations now occur, for example, on routes leading to matches or in secluded, prearranged locations (Kossakowski, 2021). One gets the impression that subsequent amendments to this law were primarily driven by political decisions, often with minimal legislative value.

The Law of 1997 underwent no less than eleven amendments within a decade of its enactment. In 2008, efforts to create a new version of the law commenced. These efforts were primarily focused on regulating football matches, with particular emphasis on combating stadium hooliganism. One of the reasons for enacting a new law was the selection (in April 2007) of Poland and Ukraine as the hosts for the UEFA European Football Championship – EURO 2012. However, similar to the situation with the 1997 law, the immediate catalyst for these efforts was a series of disturbances, notably during the Final of the Polish Cup in 2008 between Legia Warsaw and Wisła Kraków, as well as the detention of 700 Legia Warsaw supporters en route to a match (also in 2008) against Polonia Warsaw. The culmination of these events occurred in October 2008 during a match between the Polish national team and Slovakia, where, due to disturbances caused by Polish fans, 7 police officers and 60 Polish national team supporters were injured. The close succession of these events prompted the immediate establishment of a commission in November 2008, tasked with definitively addressing the issue of hooliganism at football matches involving Polish fans. The Polish Parliament ultimately passed the new Law on the Safety of Mass Events in March 2009.

The Law on the Safety of Mass Events of 2009 is characterized by greater comprehensiveness and specificity of regulations, as well as a markedly increased rigour and punitiveness, especially in relation to football matches. In this context, the responsibilities of the organizer were significantly expanded, and various entities were obligated to utilize modern technologies for securing mass events, drawing inspiration mainly from regulations in force in the United Kingdom (e.g., regarding fan identification). This Law drastically tightened the criminal sanctions for legal violations and, for the first time, introduced a new repressive measure that can be applied ex post facto – the club ban.

As of September 1, 2023, the Law on the Safety of Mass Events has been amended no less than sixteen times. In the majority of cases, the law was amended in response to incidents of antisocial behaviour occurring during football matches, which were widely covered by the mass media. For instance, changes to the Act in October 2011 were prompted by hooliganism during the Polish Cup final in May 2011 between Lech Poznań and Legia Warsaw. The parliamentary subcommittee responsible for these changes was established as early as June 2011. Consequently, most of the amendments aimed to enhance the restrictiveness of its provisions.

For example, the stadium ban procedure became a very useful tool in the fight against hooligans and drastically reduced the membership of many fan groups across the country in the next few years. In the original Law (1997), the ban on admission to a mass event was only an additional punishment imposed (very rarely in practice) for a period of between three and twelve months. As modified by the amendments (e.g., in 2009 and 2011), however, it was no longer an additional penalty but a penal measure, and the catalogue of offences for which it could be imposed was extended: apart from, for example, bringing pyrotechnics to the stadium, it also came to include, for example, using a piece of clothing or an object to cover one's face in order to prevent or hinder face recognition (introduced after the fans began to cover their faces while firing pyrotechnics and thus hindered the identification of the perpetrator). The bans have been extended, ranging from two to six years. Nowadays, the prohibition of access to a mass event also applies to a football match played by the Polish national cadre and the Polish sports club outside the territory of the Republic of Poland. Following the increasing problem with bans, fans of some clubs decided to give up supporting their team during matches played in the home stadium for some time. In the following years, football banning orders, different from the prohibition of access to mass events, became a more popular form of punishment. Practically every single round of Ekstraklasa had at least one match with no away supporters present. Moreover, the organizer can also impose the prohibition of access to football games – the outcome is that the fan must not participate in any mass event. Honestly, the private entity-organizer replaces the common court.

The introduction of more restrictive legal regulations and the fact that they became consistently enforced pushed out hooligan confrontations from the stadiums. Criminological analyses show that in recent years, there has been a clear downward trend in collective violation of the law in Polish stadiums: 'the figures recorded from 2011 onwards are among the lowest since 1997' (Drzazga, 2016: 257). The decline in the number of such incidents results from tightened control over the most fanatical groups – the hosts and the guests are most often seated in the opposite stands, the guests are closely watched by the police throughout their journey, and wait up to two hours after the match in their sector so that the home team supporters leave first. The strictness of a punishment that fans risk is another component, especially since they can no longer remain anonymous: Polish stadiums follow contemporary trends and have the most modern and effective surveillance and security systems.

Recent history clearly reveals that the law has become increasingly more restrictive and has come to affect an increasingly broader spectrum of spectators' behaviours (the phenomenon can be observed in Poland and other European countries; see Tsoukala, 2009; Doidge et al., 2020). There is no doubt that when Poland was selected as a co-host for the Euro 2012 championship, state structures began to interfere in the conduct of supporters (Antonowicz and Grodecki, 2018). From a broader perspective, hosting the championship was considered a significant reinforcement of Poland's path of modernization (Kossakowski, 2019). The national authorities and general public opinion put enormous work and attention into convincing the international audience that Poland deserves to be called a 'Western' country. The unpredictable behaviour of the 'wild' fans may have prevented the fulfilment of this historic opportunity, which is why the issue of legal restrictions on football matches became politically pressing.

The Politicization of Fandom 'Issue'

The evolution of the law dedicated to sports events and fans' behaviours can be perceived as a natural effect of changes within cultural patterns and social attitudes. It would be hard to maintain the acts implemented, for example, in the communist era, as many aspects of football fields have dramatically changed. For example, the English example shows that some – even radical – law amendments were the results of historical events. It was clearly visible in the context of the Hillsborough disaster in 1989, as a result of which national authorities implemented a series of legal solutions (as well as infrastructure ones) as a consequence of such dramatic moments. In the Polish case, it is reasonable to state that further amendments were responses to local events.

It is evident that successive tightening of regulations was linked to the behaviour of fans (typically following some incident that received extensive media coverage), with another key factor being Poland's organization of the European Championships. In the language of politicians who held power at that time, it is clear that the amendment of legislation concerning mass events was a matter concerning 'fans'. This is demonstrated, for instance, in the statement by Marek Biernacki, the Chairman of the Committee on Administration and Internal Affairs, during the amendment process:

> This law must come into force. We need to see how it will work. Surely, there will be a need for improvements. I do not believe that we will create excellent legislation right away. However, as you have noticed, work on this law is very dynamic. Therefore, it seems to us that this is a

certain minimum. All of you, the Members of Parliament, agreed on this date. We have a great challenge ahead of us in the form of Euro 2012. It would be bad if there were any riots and disturbances before 2012.
(Transcript of the Committee on Administration and Internal Affairs meeting No. 97, Bulletin No. 1742/VI)

From a retrospective standpoint, it is evident that the Law on the Safety of Mass Events, although ostensibly dedicated to various events, primarily arose from the desire to prevent the phenomenon of so-called stadium hooliganism, which is closely associated with one of the most popular contemporary sports disciplines, namely football. Unfortunately, due to their spectacular nature, these antisocial behaviours attract significant attention from the mass media, making them a focal point in political discourse. The law's focus on just one phenomenon results in difficulties for other organizers of mass events (e.g., rock concerts) in its application. Furthermore, the enactment of the Law on the Safety of Mass Events and its subsequent amendments occurred with significant involvement from the press, radio, and television, leading to haste in its adoption, which is not advisable in legislative processes.

Additionally, this situation indirectly forces a trend in which lawmakers systematically expand the scope of criminalization of specific behaviours taking place during mass events, even though the primary issue related to stadium hooliganism occurs outside of these events. Moreover, it should be noted that combating social pathologies, including those associated with stadium-related criminal activity, solely through legal and punitive measures poses numerous challenges. The phenomenon is extensive and difficult to define, making the application of solely punitive legal norms challenging and, in practical terms, nearly impossible. In the context of legal changes in Poland, there has been no mention of alternative means to counter violence in stadiums, such as implementing special social and educational programmes aimed at socializing younger generations of fans towards more positive fan behaviour patterns.

The haste in implementing legislative changes had legal consequences, as a highly controversial law was adopted, some of whose provisions contradict the fundamental law – the constitution (Warchoł, 2012). To a large extent, the Law on the Safety of Mass Events was enacted to fulfil the constitutional obligation of ensuring safety and public order by the state. However, many times, the provisions of this act violate other provisions of the Polish Constitution. What is significant is that this act contains norms from various legal fields, which often leads to practical challenges due to differences in the interpretation of individual legal fields. Furthermore, the legislative work is rightly criticized in doctrine for its lack of precision – for instance, linguistic errors appeared in the text of the law. Therefore, the character of the law can be described by the statement: 'The end justifies the means'.

However, for the political authorities of that time, the key objective was to introduce a law that would serve as a response to alleged threats to public order from hooligans and simultaneously address the media uproar concerning acts of hooliganism in stadiums. The Polish government took the UEFA European Championship 2012 opportunity seriously, and the stringent law was meant to guarantee 'peace', even at the cost of legal and constitutional uncertainties. Nevertheless, politicians believed that public opinion expected such 'decisive' solutions.

It should be emphasized that acts of vandalism and hooliganism did occur in Polish stadiums at the time. The incidents of vandalism, which were publicized by the media, definitely played an important role in the decision-making process. One of the incidents was the riots after the Polish Cup Finals in 2011 (fans of Lech Poznań and Legia Warsaw clashed with police and security and demolished the stadium). After this match, Prime Minister Donald Tusk announced an uncompromising campaign against stadium hooligans:

> Even if the struggle for peace and security for people in the stadiums is going to take weeks, (...) or months, as of today, we will not step back an inch. (...) This struggle must bring results as soon as possible, and the victory must be on the side of decent people who want to watch matches and not brawls in the stadiums, people who do not want to listen to the endless stream of verbal abuse. (...) This war can be won.
> (Premier idzie na wojnę ... 2011)

Politicians clearly mapped out the difference between 'civilized people and those who behave contrary to the expected norms: 'Poland has more important problems today than the comfort of those who want to riot in the stadiums. For those who disrupt order, there is no alternative: the state must be ruthless in law enforcement' (*Kibice i premier* ... 2011). Politicians' opinions about supporters went hand in hand with media discourses which involved the use of such terms as 'bandits', 'rogues', 'hordes', 'stadium bandits', 'aggressive adolescents in tracksuits', 'stadium hordes', 'fascists' and even 'terrorists' (Kossakowski, 2021). Following the rhetoric of Prime Minister Tusk, the minister of internal affairs in his government stated in 2013: 'We are dealing with the savagery of a part of society. (...) either *kibole* will get socialized, or other solutions will need to be applied' (*Sienkiewicz zapowiada* ... nd). Media supporting the government published articles that stigmatized the behaviour of fans and created a moral panic about them (Woźniak, 2013).

(Ineffective) Fans' Resistance

As might be expected, when the greatest legal restrictions were being introduced and the media vilified, supporters tried to voice their opposition. Fan actions reached their peak in 2011. The most famous slogan presented in match choreographies at several stadiums was 'Donald, you moron, fans will bring your government down'; another one was: 'Project Euro 2012 – stadiums: overpaid; highways: won't be there; railway stations: a splash of paint; airports: provincial; players: weak; red herring: football fans; the government: satisfied'. The antagonistic attitude towards the government contributed to the strengthening of the fans' collective identity. Supporters of different clubs, generally divided by internal animosities, spoke with one voice in the face of growing repression. The sense of discrimination and victimization could significantly impact the process of reconstructing the identity politics of Polish supporters.

However, as time has shown, the mobilization of resources within the fan community did not yield significant results. Fans possessed an unprecedented power – for instance, they could have organized a nationwide boycott of league matches. Since the attendance at league matches in Poland was not very high at that time, and it was mainly determined by the most devoted fans, their boycott could have had a substantial impact on the situation's development. Faced with the loss of a significant number of fans, clubs might have engaged in discussions about the legal problem of restrictions. Such civil disobedience by fans could have shaken Polish football and possibly compelled politicians to reconsider their actions. However, this did not happen. The unity among fans essentially boiled down to chanting slogans in stadiums and preparing occasional banners. Their common 'antagonistic' identity did not acquire significant institutional expressions. Although fans of many clubs established a common umbrella organization in 2007 called the National Union of Supporters' Associations (*Ogólnopolski Związek Stowarzyszeń Kibicowskich*) and intended to integrate fans in the struggle for their interests (providing institutional evidence of their integration), this organization was unable to harness the strength and potential of fans from across Poland to build a united front against the changes taking place in Poland. Today, there is no trace of its activity.

In the face of legal, media, and political pressure, the fan community proved to be powerless. The main reasons for this state of affairs were primarily local circumstances and interests in which fans of individual clubs were involved. It is not a secret that organized groups of fans cooperate with the authorities of their clubs, and both sides benefit from such a coalition: the clubs' authorities have the assurance of maintaining order, for example, in the ultras section, while fans can earn money, for example, from catering or fans souvenirs sales. Involvement in a nationwide boycott could disrupt these 'business' relationships and even drastically limit them. It turned out that fighting for the 'fan cause' would lead to a conflict of 'interests'.

As a consequence of this fact, every change in the law and the decisions of football authorities in Poland were implemented without consulting fans and with their passive acceptance. The only reaction from fans to external factors was chants in the stands and banners. However, these actions had no significant impact and were merely the 'swan song' of this community.

The following words from a Legia Warsaw fan aptly illustrate how successive changes in the law and procedures were 'accepted' by the fan community:

> We let them push the limits ... In the 1990s, you had to invade the pitch. There had to be fifty injured or an abandoned match to make the sort of story in the papers you can read today when just a single flare has been fired. And back then, to make a good headline, you had to call those who invaded the pitch bandits; that's why some smaller things, I mean, smaller fights, were not really noticed, and that's why they were seen as a norm. Today, they close stands or the whole stadiums for choreographies and flares. Back then, it really had to be something big to do that. Like the stadium set on fire at the Legia vs. Wisła match back in 2001, it was just a fight between Wisła guys and the police in their sector, and fire set in ours; they called the fire brigade to put it out. I think that was the sort of thing that made them close the stand, and it was only for two matches. And today ... [Interview by one of the authors]

Conclusions

The history of transformations in Polish football after 1989 is, like other areas of social life, in a sense, a reflection of the transformation of society as a whole. Attempts to reconcile the new economic and political reality, new (primarily Western) institutional and cultural patterns, and old habits and legal frameworks in Polish football were not without problems. This is evident in the changes in the law dedicated to sporting events.

Fourteen years of the Law on the Safety of Mass Events in force allow us to conclude that a separate law on the safety and organization of football matches should be enacted in the Polish legal system. This is because some of the obligations established in the first of the mentioned laws essentially pertain only to this category of events. Therefore, it is imperative to enact a new version of the law on the safety of mass events and separate from it the provisions concerning football because subsequent changes to it do not positively affect the quality of its content. The law described in the article contains numerous inaccuracies and even linguistic errors; hence, it should be enacted anew. Furthermore, football-related crime can now be described as 'around the stadium' rather than strictly 'stadium-based' because, as a result of the law and modern stadium infrastructure, fights among hooligans occur outside stadium grounds.

In the Polish context, it is increasingly important to emphasize the economic aspect. Polish football does not belong to the top leagues in Europe – it can be considered part of the semi-peripheral leagues (as reflected, for example, in the UEFA rankings). However, it is clear visible that modernization processes are changing Polish football, from youth training to the media coverage of matches. The organization of football matches constitutes an economic activity that is in a phase of systematic growth. This industry has become the subject of interest for leading mass media, businesses, and even politics. The course of competitions is increasingly broadcast on television stations. There is no doubt that in the coming years, the developmental trend of mass events will continue. Therefore, it is important to consider the fight against violence in stadiums in the context of the commercialization processes of football. These processes, for example, lead to the emergence of 'new' fans, such as families with children. The appropriate legal framework should serve to create a sense of security for all participants in a football match. However, it should not penalize behaviours that are associated with a more passionate way of supporting one's favourite club. We believe that a football match should be a space for fulfilment for various types of fans. Hasty implementation of laws driven by short-term political interests does not serve this purpose.

Note

1 In Poland, the first antisocial behaviours, mainly during football matches, were already noted in the mid-1970s. In May 1980, massive clashes occurred between fans of Lech Poznań and Legia Warsaw during the final of the Polish Cup, which took place in Częstochowa. On May 29, 1993, before the Poland-England match in Chorzów, a fan of Pogoń Szczecin was fatally stabbed by a Cracovia Kraków fan, and the match itself at Stadion Śląski essentially constituted a 90-minute regular battle between participants of this mass event. Therefore, the legislative inaction in this regard is quite astonishing. See more in P. Piotrowski, *Szalikowcy*, p. 31; C. Kąkol, Bezpieczeństwo imprez masowych (Safety of Mass Events), 2012, p. 22.

References

Antonowicz, D & Grodecki, M (2018) Missing the goal: Policy evolution towards football-related violence in Poland (1989–2012). *International Review for the Sociology of Sport* 53(4), 490–511.

Antonowicz, D, Kossakowski, R, and Szlendak, T (2015) *Aborygeni i konsumenci. O kibicowskiej wspólnocie, komercjalizacji futbolu i stadionowym apartheidzie*. Warszawa. IFiS PAN.

Carlsson, B & Backman, J (2023) Juridification of fandom: Dealing with spectators' expressions of 'too much joy' in Swedish football. *Soccer & Society* 24(3), 364–377.

Crabbe, T & Brown, A (2004) You're not welcome anymore: The football crowd, class and social exclusion. In: Wagg, S (ed) *Football and Social Exclusion*. London. Routledge, pp. 71–81.

Doidge, M, Kossakowski, R & Mintert, S (2020) *Ultras: The Passion and Performance of Contemporary Football Fandom*. Manchester. Manchester University Press.

Dróżdż, M (2014) Security of sports events in Poland – Polish act on mass events security. *Ius Novum* 2, 171–185.

Dróżdż, M (2020) *Ustawa o bezpieczeństwie imprez masowych. Komentarz*. Warszawa. Beck.

Drzazga, E (2016) *Chuligaństwo stadionowe w Polsce. Studium z zakresu kontroli społecznej zjawiska*. Warszawa. Scholar.

Flint, J & Powell, R (2014) 'We've got the equivalent of Passchendaele': Sectarianism, football and urban disorder in Scotland. In: Hopkins, M & Treadwell, J (eds) *Football Hooliganism, Fan Behaviour and Crime. Contemporary Issues*. Basingstoke. Palgrave Macmillan, pp. 71–91.

Giulianotti, R (1994) Social identity and public order: Political and academic discourses on football violence. In: Giulianotti, R, Bonney, N & Hepworth, M (eds) *Football, Violence and Social Identity*. London. Routledge, pp. 9–36.

Giulianotti, R (2011) Sport mega events, urban football carnivals and securitised commodification: The case of the English Premier League. Urban Studies 48(15), 3293–3310.

Hopkins, M & Treadwell, J (eds) (2014) Football Hooliganism, Fan Behaviour and Crime. Contemporary Issues. Basingstoke. Palgrave Macmillan.

Kąkol, C (2012) *Bezpieczeństwo imprez masowych. Komentarz*. Warszawa. Kluver.

Kossakowski, R (2019) Euro 2012, the 'civilizational leap' and the 'supporters United' programme: A football mega-event and the evolution of fan culture in Poland. *Soccer and Society* 20(5), 729–743.

Kossakowski, R (2021) *Hooligans, Ultras, Activists. Polish Football Fandom in Sociological Perspective*. Cham. Palgrave Macmillan.

Piotrowski, P (1999) *Szalikowcy. O zachowaniach dewiacyjnych kibiców sportowych*. Toruń. Marszałek.

Tsoukala, A (2009) *Football Hooliganism in Europe. Security and Civil Liberties in the Balance*. Basingstoke. Palgrave Macmillan.

Turner, M (2022) The Safe Standing movement in English football: Mobilizing across the political and discursive fields of contention. *Current Sociology* 70(7), 1048–1065.

Waiton, S (2014) Football fans in an Age of Intolerance. In Hopkins, M & Treadwell, J (eds) *Football Hooliganism, Fan Behaviour and Crime. Contemporary Issues*. Basingstoke. Palgrave Macmillan, pp. 201–221.

Warchoł, M (2012) Konstytucyjne problemy bezpieczeństwa imprez masowych, Przegląd. *Legislacyjny* 2, 1–14.

Woźniak, W (2013) O użyteczności koncepcji paniki moralnej jako ramy analitycznej dla badań nad zjawiskiem przemocy około futbolowej. In: Kossakowski, R, Stachura, K, Strzałkowska, A, and Żadkowska, M (eds) *Futbol i cała reszta. Sport w perspektywie nauk społecznych*. Pszczółki. Wydawnictwo Orbis Exterior, pp. 248–267.

3 Modern Football and Social Spacing

Ian Woolsey

Contested Spaces

From its humble origins as a 'folk' game, through to the establishment of the English Football Association in 1863 and beyond, football spaces have operated both as sites of social exclusion and homes for contrasting styles of support (see Russell, 1997).[1] Arguably however, debates about appropriate supporter behaviour went into overdrive in the wake of the post-1989 transformation of English football. Advanced surveillance techniques (Crawford, 2004), all seater-stadia (Crabbe and Brown, 2004), rising ticket prices (Conn, 1997), and a growing intolerance to expressive modes of fandom (see Parry and Malcolm, 2004), have all transformed the experience of watching the professional game. These modifications have, as Sandvoss (2003) suggests, been accompanied by a growth in the sport's popularity, its appeal now traversing some of the more traditional boundaries of class, age, geography, and gender. However, not every supporter has welcomed these changes with open arms, some clinging steadfastly to a perceived set of 'authentic' practices (see King, 1998).

Drawing on Bauman's (1993: 145) ideas about social spacing, this chapter will discuss the efforts which travelling supporters make to control social space and defend their lifeworld from the modernisation of English football. Expressed succinctly, for Bauman (1993: 145), the first of these three 'interwoven, yet distinct' processes; *cognitive* spacing, is a function of knowledge control. It draws lines between those who are 'in' and those who are 'out', based upon their level of biographical familiarity. By contrast, the second process which Bauman describes, *moral* spacing, is concerned with who we live 'for', rather than simply 'with'. It is altruistic, impulsive, and emotional. It cares little for rational calculation, depersonalised rules, and opportunities for personal reward. The final process which completes Bauman's model, *aesthetic spacing*, has no love for such moral fortitude. Rather, its steering principles are amusement, freedom, and novelty. Driven by curiosity and a search for experiential intensity, aesthetic spacing offers entrance into a world which is dreamlike and hazy, its ethereal promises seducing all those who have grown weary of the grounded mundanity of the working week. However, there are several occasions when these different types of spacing are complementary, rather than antithetical. The chapter will now discuss the interpretive character of the English football 'community'.

Decoding the Football Community

Association football, whose rules were formally inaugurated in 1863, is a distinctly modern phenomenon. As such, any 'community' which we might associate with this sport is, by its very nature, an *interpretive* one. The reason for this can be traced to the transformation of community, which accompanied the onset of modernity sometime during the 1600s. Blackshaw (2010: 26) suggests that in contrast to its pre-modern counterpart, the modern world is not predicated upon the axis of a 'singular community', 'the *arché*, or the underlying source of the being of all things human'. Rather, what can be inferred is that community, and by extension, what it means to be human, is now a fluid and negotiable construct. Not only did 'freedom', that great pillar of modernity (see Delanty, 1999), rob this pre-modern steering mechanism of its co-ordinating powers; it also cast the modern world into an endless cycle of transformation. One outcome of this, suggests Blackshaw (2010: 27), is an unabashed *nostalgia* for community. A second outcome is a determination among the modern populace to give this entity meaning.

Significantly, as Bauman (2001a: 12) suggests, 'Spoken of' ... community ... 'is a contradiction in terms'. To articulate community is to recognise its inoperative character, that is, to draw attention to a paucity of *shared* understandings. Communities which exist 'matter of factly' explains Bauman, do not require their members to track them down, nor are they required to fight for the intersubjective understanding which underpin them. Rather, this understanding is a given. That football supporters are able to speak so readily about their 'community' is testament to the discord that exists among the English football 'community' (supporters, owners, legislators) at large. Such a development is reflected by, and necessitates, an abandonment of the tacitly experienced 'natural attitude' (Schutz, 1970), shifting the football 'community' away from its *pre-reflective* backstage role and placing it onto centre stage. If this is common to all modern communities, then its relevance to football supporters has become *exceptional*. Ever since the architects of (post-1989) modern football tore up the existing templates and designs for living which had been utilised by previous generations who, predominantly, operated in the 'practical attitude', the 'taken for granted character' of these supporters' activities, is now anything but that. Rather, their orientation is increasingly reflective; their attitude 'theoretical' (Schutz, 1971: 208) rather than 'practical'. The chapter will now discuss these supporters' hermeneutic practices and the cognitive forms of spacing which they engage in to seek control.

Cognitive Spacing and 'Authenticity'

Generally speaking, the hermeneutic community that provided the focus for my (2021) research, express a desire for a return to the 'good old days', a return to the *automated* character of the 'natural attitude' (Schutz, 1970). However, first the war which it wishes to leave behind must be won. Struggles regarding 'authentic' football support (even if these are the magical product of an earnest imagination) are central to this battle. Victory must be absolute. This persuasion was captured well by 'Sid', who recalled an encounter with the 'pioneer' behind the introduction of all-seated stadiums in top-flight English football, Lord Justice Taylor. Despite agreeing with Taylor's downbeat assessment of the facilities at Millwall's Old Den stadium, what the participant did not share with this influential figure was his disdain for the joys of standing and its associated aesthetic properties. Positioning himself as a knowledgeable actor, the participant suggested:

'Sid': He said, 'You can hardly see a thing in here … If you were going to the theatre your ticket would say you have got a restricted view'. What he did not understand, him not being a football person, [is] that … going to a football match is not quite like going to The Crucible[2] … the atmosphere's completely different.

And here lays the crux of the matter: from the perspective of several 'traditional supporters', the architects of the post-1989 modernisation of English football are steering this popular pastime down the path to cultural Armageddon. Drinking, swearing, and standing (see Turner and Ludvigsen, 2022) have become the activities of the pariahs of the new visionaries: old-fashioned relics that need to be extinguished to complete the gentrified cosmetic overhaul. The tools of surveillance provide the necessary means of violence, and the moral discourses the justification for their use. Whereas football grounds (or at least sections of them) once provided a safe haven for the 'natural attitude', a chance to remain switched off in the company of likeminded individuals, now, what Wittgenstein (cited in Bauman, 2001b: 33) would refer to as a 'knowledge of how to go on' has become more uncertain in this domain.

Disturbed by the incursion of these cognitive strangers, football's 'traditional' supporters have sought to defend their lifeworld from this type of boundary encroachment via what Bauman (1993) refers to as 'phagic' (inclusivist) and 'emic' (exclusivist) strategies. The mantra is simple: 'conform or be damned', 'play the game by our rules' (Bauman, 1993: 163) or we will toss you over the castle walls and raise the drawbridge forever. Correspondingly, hope springs eternal for all those who are willing to lay down their weapons and open their arms to the phagically loaded forms of salvation which are brought to the negotiating table:

Gaz: They patently only ever [go to] home games, they are there with their flask or whatever … but I'd love to get them by the hand and take them to an away game and say, 'Look this is really what your clubs all about'… I think everybody should go to an away game. If you haven't, you will never really truly understand.

The words 'truly understand' are significant here and emphasise the exclusionary, cognitively fuelled character of belonging. Gaz's words also highlight the mutually interdependent relationship between 'phagic' and 'emic' strategies. 'Come with us, let us lead you down the path towards enlightenment', goes the mantra, 'otherwise you will stay in your poorly illuminated cave for the rest of your days', a real-life working replica of Plato's shadow-watchers.

Moral Spacing

Social spacing is not reducible to the configuration of the cognitive domain; moral spacing also has a hand to play in the overall organisation of the cultural sphere. In the last instance, moral spacing is concerned with the individuals who 'we live *for*', meaning that the objects of concern are of a different character to those in the cognitive space, that is, those who 'we live *with*' (Bauman, 1993: 165). Digging a deeper trench between the two space-making processes, Bauman develops his argument by insisting that the objects of moral spacing are immune to the processes of typification which reside in the cognitive domain. That is to say, the selection of appropriate objects for our attention in this sphere is guided by moral concerns, rather than categorical membership. Being a fully paid-up member of the cognitive guild does not guarantee entry into the moral clubhouse so to speak. This has important implications for the operation of power within a football environment.

What Is Moral Action?

In his 1993 treatise, *Postmodern Ethics*, Bauman outlines the failure of humankind to establish a set of universally applicable ethical principles. Having done so, Bauman sets out his own vision of how the term 'morality' should properly be understood. The conclusion which Bauman arrives at is important as it allows for a more nuanced understanding of football supporter behaviour than that which is sometimes presented.

The first point which Bauman (1993) wishes to make is that morality is not founded upon a set of symmetrical relationships. When humans genuinely act *for* the other, they do so without an expectation of 'reciprocation' or 'reward'. 'Indifference' (1993: 48) to the actions of the other is a hallmark of morality. Put simply, the actor who is 'for', is so, regardless of the willingness of the recipients to return the favour. Drawing on the ideas of Levinas, Bauman elevates the moral actor above and beyond the business-like partners whose actions rotate around the fulfilment of a set of mutually binding (externally enforceable) contractual *obligations*. The burden of the moral actor suggests Bauman, is not one which is shared by the masses, but rather is one which is endured 'alone'. These responsibilities are out of the ordinary, rather than 'statistically average'. Common standards which would deny the individual their uniqueness and shared ideals which emanate from a collective identity are not the stuff of which moral action is made. Too bad it might be assumed, for

committed to production decreased. The world's population was growing, and European settlers in particular were scouting the globe for ever more contiguous settlements. New transportation technologies, in particular, the steamship and railway, not only transformed the world of markets but also increased human mobility and, not least, created the infrastructural basis for the emerging middle-class tourism industry. And tourism in turn, through a dialectical process, increased the demand for "unspoiled nature," which justified its provision. Scientific exploration and topographic surveying of the world helped to remove the last blank spots from the increasingly ubiquitous maps. At the beginning of the twentieth century, only the poles and a few mountain peaks had not yet been explored by Europeans. In the apt yet trenchant words of the French geographer Jean Brunhes, penned in 1909, "the limits of our cage" had been reached.[32]

Second, a new perception of nature had been emerging since the late eighteenth century. Romanticism ushered in an aesthetic appreciation of nature and turned it into a moral issue. Jean-Jacques Rousseau and others became pioneers of a new way of looking at nature, which sees nature as both the physical basis of life and as having an intrinsic value that liberates nature and engages with it. Outdoor experiences took on a transcendental quality and were perceived as enriching and morally uplifting. Mountain or coastal landscapes that previously had received little attention—and then, most often as barriers to traffic—became worthy travel destinations in themselves. Aside from philosophy, the natural sciences, too, were busy constructing a new perception of nature. In the 1800s, the Christian story of creation, which had shaped the image of nature in Europe for centuries, came under pressure. Scientific discoveries and findings, especially Charles Darwin's epochal *Origin of Species* in 1859, were increasingly less compatible with biblical tradition. The world was evidently not only much older than previously thought, it had also changed significantly over time. This insight increased interest in the history of nature and of places where such history could be studied. These destinations acquired the aura of shrines, and the spirituality found in nature had the power to replace the creeds and services associated with the bible and religious bodies. Nonetheless, Christian belief and the new appreciation of nature often came together and were expressed through the sacralization of the Alps in the nineteenth century, when one peak after another was adorned with a cross.[33]

Third, the new interest in nature did not spread evenly within society. Rather, natural ethics and the natural sciences flourished in a specific milieu that took shape simultaneously in the industrializing Western countries: the urban educated middle class.[34] From this stratum came the great majority of thinkers and scientists who revolutionized the image of nature and later also supported the conservation movement. In addition to its enlightened attitude, this social stratum also acquired a degree of prosperity that allowed its members to pursue ideas beyond those concerned with meeting basic needs. The educated classes that we encounter in the history of conservation did not stop at their personal studies of nature; they read Rousseau and Darwin and met up in scientific societies. They reveled in nature and developed through their scientific excursions a keen sense for changes in the landscape. Nature conservation found the objects of its desire in peripheral rural areas, whereas its elites and its base came from urban households.

The fourth and final interpretive strand is the process of establishing territories, which took on a new character with imperialism and the building of nation-states.[35] On the one hand, the existing colonial powers and countries aspiring to the global stage, such as Germany, Italy, the United States, and Japan (and, rather bizarrely, the Belgian king) not only nearly completely divided the world among themselves; they also tried, with the aid of modern science and technology, to bind their old and new colonies more strongly to the colonial center and to bring them under their rule. On the other hand, nation-states gave rise to government territories that became an important reference point for the formation of national identity. In the common space "imagined communities" became rooted.[36] Biological determinism allowed deduction of national characteristics from the living space, and the national community could be founded in natural history. The geographical unity of the country virtually guaranteed the unique character of the population.[37] As already mentioned, this model of identity had its fullest effect in nations that possessed few measurable commonalities. In the United States, the national parks were "vignettes of primitive America," whereas in Switzerland their purpose was to create spaces in which "Old Helvetia" could rise again.[38]

The Global Conservation Movement

All these processes continued to have an effect for many decades. In contrast, nature conservation as an organized movement arose within only a relatively short period of time—less than a generation. Between 1890 and 1914, in Europe, North America, and among the white populations of European colonies, associations formed and pledged themselves to the cause of preserving nature. Although at its founding in 1891, the Sierra Club stood more or less alone, by 1910 the United States boasted around twenty nature conservation organizations.[39] The United Kingdom saw the founding of the National Trust in 1895 and the Society for the Preservation of the Wild Fauna of the Empire in 1903. And at the turn of the century, on the European continent, conservation organizations emerged in quick succession. The German *Bund für Vogelschutz* and the German-Austrian *Verein Naturschutzpark,* the French *Société pour la Protection des Paysages,* the Dutch *Vereeniging tot Behoud van Natuurmonu-*

committed to production decreased. The world's population was growing, and European settlers in particular were scouting the globe for ever more contiguous settlements. New transportation technologies, in particular, the steamship and railway, not only transformed the world of markets but also increased human mobility and, not least, created the infrastructural basis for the emerging middle-class tourism industry. And tourism in turn, through a dialectical process, increased the demand for "unspoiled nature," which justified its provision. Scientific exploration and topographic surveying of the world helped to remove the last blank spots from the increasingly ubiquitous maps. At the beginning of the twentieth century, only the poles and a few mountain peaks had not yet been explored by Europeans. In the apt yet trenchant words of the French geographer Jean Brunhes, penned in 1909, "the limits of our cage" had been reached.[32]

Second, a new perception of nature had been emerging since the late eighteenth century. Romanticism ushered in an aesthetic appreciation of nature and turned it into a moral issue. Jean-Jacques Rousseau and others became pioneers of a new way of looking at nature, which sees nature as both the physical basis of life and as having an intrinsic value that liberates nature and engages with it. Outdoor experiences took on a transcendental quality and were perceived as enriching and morally uplifting. Mountain or coastal landscapes that previously had received little attention—and then, most often as barriers to traffic—became worthy travel destinations in themselves. Aside from philosophy, the natural sciences, too, were busy constructing a new perception of nature. In the 1800s, the Christian story of creation, which had shaped the image of nature in Europe for centuries, came under pressure. Scientific discoveries and findings, especially Charles Darwin's epochal *Origin of Species* in 1859, were increasingly less compatible with biblical tradition. The world was evidently not only much older than previously thought, it had also changed significantly over time. This insight increased interest in the history of nature and of places where such history could be studied. These destinations acquired the aura of shrines, and the spirituality found in nature had the power to replace the creeds and services associated with the bible and religious bodies. Nonetheless, Christian belief and the new appreciation of nature often came together and were expressed through the sacralization of the Alps in the nineteenth century, when one peak after another was adorned with a cross.[33]

Third, the new interest in nature did not spread evenly within society. Rather, natural ethics and the natural sciences flourished in a specific milieu that took shape simultaneously in the industrializing Western countries: the urban educated middle class.[34] From this stratum came the great majority of thinkers and scientists who revolutionized the image of nature and later also supported the conservation movement. In addition to its enlightened attitude, this social stratum also acquired a degree of prosperity that allowed its mem-

who swear in front of women and children, Richard's disapproval of pestering female railway passengers who have no interest in being 'chatted up', Nick's decision to challenge the supporters who had called a steward a 'cunt' as he tried to explain a turnstile malfunction which had delayed their entry into the stadium, can all be categorised as autonomous moral acts. These decisive acts dismantle, or perhaps better, disturb the coherence of cognitive spacing, but it must be remembered that for every 'hero', there are often countless 'villains', or perhaps less incriminatingly, those who take an amoral, rather than an immoral stance.

Aesthetic Spacing

So far, this chapter has discussed the importance of cognitive spacing in providing a 'home' for travelling football supporters and the role which moral spacing plays in disturbing their cognitive coherence. The chapter concludes by discussing a third type of spacing – 'aesthetic' – which is motivated *primarily* by different concerns to its moral and cognitive counterparts. 'Plotted affectively, by the attention guided by curiosity and the search for experiential intensity' (Bauman, 1993: 146), aesthetic spacing is the outcome of playful endeavour, a release valve for the human spirit, in what otherwise largely amounts to a fettered social existence. Correspondingly, the wellsprings of aesthetic spacing are experiential intensity, amusement, novelty, and freedom, rather than the instinctual *moral* urges described earlier.

It is worth clarifying that the term 'aesthetics' is not used here to refer exclusively to visual or artistic beauty, but rather and following MacDougall (1999), is defined more broadly to capture those *sensate-emotional* pleasures which can be derived from one's environment and/or 'a specific cultural form or social situation' (Boyne, cited in Giulianotti, 1999: 53). Importantly and in the context of travelling football supporters' attempts to defend a perceived 'authentic' mode of fandom, this chapter focuses not only on the *passive* consumption of these types of pleasure, but also on those which football supporters *actively* produce. One outcome of their endeavours is a rich aesthetic experience above and beyond that which can be found at home games.

Experiential Intensity

Few experiences in life can provide the intensity and the cathartic properties of being among a raucous football crowd; the noise, vibrancy, colour, and sheer burst of emotion, can all play their part in, to borrow from Elias and Dunning (1986: 72), periodically refreshing 'the soul'. The playful endeavour and *imaginative* performances of football supporters play a central role in generating the atmospheric intensity which can be found within football stadiums around the world, whether these actions take the form of a carefully stage-managed performance, as is the case when Borussia Dortmund fans collaborate to produce their infamous 'Big Yellow Wall' or rely on something more spontaneous. However, the modernising football environment in which football supporters operate, presents a series of obstacles which must be tackled if they are to realise their ambitions. These include (although this list is not exhaustive) prohibitions on standing, the use of pyrotechnics, restrictions which limit free movement, and the consumption of alcohol. These themes provide the focus for the remainder of the chapter.

Standing and Pyros

Football 'places' generate debate about their appearance, their underlying meanings, and the specific aesthetic sensations which one should expect to experience when visiting these locales. Correspondingly, altercations can arise when supporters choose to ignore specific directives which threaten to curtail their performance – the desire to organise social space along *aesthetic* lines often clashing with the *moral* imperative to protect the rights of all. Chief among these is the demand which some stewards make for supporters to sit down, non-compliance sometimes resulting in ejection from the stadium or in more extreme cases, arrest. In the context of travelling football supporters this is especially pertinent, given their propensity in most cases to stand for the duration of the game. However, it is worth noting that *moral* concerns can also influence the willingness of supporters to comply with these dictates. Drawing attention to the exclusionary character of this specific practice which decreases the visibility for some supporters of events which are taking place on the pitch, one supporter posed the question:

Sid: It's fine if you are able to do it, but what about the social mix? What about the kids, do they not matter, you know? ... What about elderly people?

Additional practices which generate aesthetic intensity have also been contested. Not without good reason, the unauthorised use of pyrotechnics (which combine both colour and sound) has long since been outlawed at football matches in the United Kingdom under the Sporting Events Act, 1985. Consequently, police sniffer dogs and bodily searches have been utilised to prevent their use. However, this has not prevented some supporters from smuggling these objects into football stadiums to fill the air with the colour of their favourite football team. Such a practice can be observed with much greater regularity at some sports stadiums in Europe, where the mantra 'no pyro, no party', has sparked the blue touchpaper for many a festivity. However, the potential of these combustible objects to cause injury has triggered alarm in some quarters. No doubt mindful of the various health conditions which renders some supporters more susceptible to their harmful substances, Chief Constable Bernard Higgins prophesised that it is 'only a matter of time before somebody gets seriously injured or, heaven forbid, killed' (Goodlad, 2018). Nevertheless, and despite the concerted efforts of various constabularies to eradicate this dangerous practice, some supporters continue to prioritise aesthetic concerns ahead of moral ones.

The importance which supporters attach to these aesthetic sensations lends credence to Bauman's (1993: 168) assertion that, 'Aesthetically the city space is a spectacle, in which the amusement value overrides all other considerations'. For all their loyalty and love of expressive support, there are occasions when the paucity of aesthetic pleasures on the pitch, chip away at the *cognitive* foundations of these supporters. A common solution to this potentially problematic situation is to use Richard's expression, to 'build something' else around the match itself. Typically, that 'something' else translates as a day out on the beer with 'the lads' and an associated quest for freedom.

Freedom

Regardless of whether travelling football supporters follow Liverpool, Barcelona, Real Madrid, or York City, the one thing they do share is a desire for freedom. However, the decision to bathe in the ethereal and hazy world of the 'leisure-life' (Blackshaw, 2003), should not simply be interpreted as hedonic (see Jones, cited in Russell, 1997) or even as a form of relaxation (see Bramham and Wagg, 2014). If it is beneficial to see leisure as the antipathy of work, an opportunity to unlock the doorway to freedom and throw off the straight jacket of the working week, then what is being described here is an opportunity to experience, however temporarily, one facet of what it means to be human. That is to take a glimpse at what life might be like, were it not for all the innumerable barriers that prevent this state from ever becoming synonymous with the human condition. The consumption of alcohol, of course, plays a central role in this emancipation.

Freedom and Drinking

In one of his earliest publications, *'The Birth of Tragedy'*, Nietzsche (2000: 19) discusses the relationship between two artistic 'drives'; the 'Apollonian', and the 'Dionysian' (named respectively after the Greek gods of 'music and poetry' and 'wine' – Rojek, 1995: 80). Whereas the former is characterised by 'measured restraint' and 'freedom from wilder impulses' (Nietzsche, 2000: 21), the latter, is associated with the 'reconciliation' of 'man', with 'nature in its estranged, hostile or subjugated forms' (ibid.: 22). Nietzsche suggests that both the 'analogy of *intoxication*', whether this relates to the consumption of 'narcotic drink' or the joys brought on by the arrival of spring, provide a useful conceptual tool for facilitating comprehension of the character of the Dionysian. However, there is something much deeper at work in Nietzsche's writings than a gratuitous advocacy of life's more carnal pleasures.

Nietzsche (2000: 22) suggests that insight into 'the essence of the Dionysian' can be derived by contemplating the 'blissful rapture' which accompanies the breakdown of the 'principium individuationis', that is, *where the structured distinctions between humans and their world begin to collapse.* 'Tango's' recollection of a day out with a group of (non-Sheffield Wednesday) supporters from the south coast of England, indicates that a love of Dionysian pleasures is not the exclusive property of the Owls travelling faithful. By itself, this 'finding' is hardly revelatory given the central place which drinking occupies in the lifeworld of this collective as a whole (see King, 1998). However, Tango's references to the kind of connectivity which accompanies the deconstruction of the 'principium individuationis', where humans begin to reconnect with one another and the world, are more thought-provoking. This renowned Sheffield Wednesday and England 'super-fan' began his vignette by describing how he had been invited to rendezvous at a public house, only to realise upon arrival that the friend who he was supposed to be meeting had got his mobile telephone switched off. Having decided to knock on the door of this (presumably secret) location Tango was met with a disconcerting silence. With hope fading fast, and fearing a stitch-up, Tango made one last-ditch attempt to join the party:

Tango: I can hear this noise, so, I bang on the door, *this arm's come and grabbed me*[4], pulled me in this pub … and I didn't buy another one … so I've gone to the bar … and this bloke's gone … 'Do you want a Jager Bomb?' Eight o'clock in the morning!

It is during this type of episode which Tango describes that society's structural properties begin to lose their influence, offering their fugitives a glimpse of 'a 'nature' that has long since become 'estranged' (Nietzsche, 2000: 22). The norms of social etiquette, the rules of language, the hierarchical relationships that divide and rule, surrender to the Authoritarian Personality (see Adorno et al., 1950), money, rank and file, none of these things have the same potency when 'supporters' are in 'their' world. The great feeling of togetherness which accompanies these encounters, the sense, to use Matt's expression, of being on a shared 'mission', cannot be found within the structured confines of 'real' or 'ordinary' (Huizinga, 2014: 8) life. Rather, it is only with the collapse of the *principium individuationis*, where the structured distinctions between humans and their world lose their currency and are temporarily declared bankrupt, that individuals can begin to experience this level of connectivity.

However, not every member of the public derives pleasure from the drunken 'communal' antics of travelling football supporters. Consequently, the British police/footballing authorities make frequent attempts to bring the party to an end, whether that be through the implementation of alcohol restrictions within the stadium or transport heading to and from the match. Suffice to say that supporters have been known to circumnavigate these prohibitions by smuggling alcohol (and illegal substances) into these locales. With variable degrees of success, the police use of sniffer dogs and body searches constitutes a counter-offensive against these forbidden practices; a tactical move in the seemingly endless game of 'cat and mouse'.

It is also worth noting that not every travelling supporter revels in the machismo of an alpha-male orientation, many gaining aesthetic pleasure from the novel environments which they seek out on a match day. The following subsection focuses on this search for the *unfamiliar* (Bauman, 1993) and the policing practices which present a thorn-in-the-side of these would-be executioners of aesthetic spacing.

Freedom and Novelty

What is an 'away day' if not a novel experience? The search for new grounds, new landscapes, and new faces, all add to the enjoyment of this activity. Strolling like Baudelaire's flaneur (see Bauman, 1993) around unfamiliar cities, taking in the smells and sounds of untried public houses, sampling the local ales, and bantering with rival supporters – people we have never met before and in all probability, will never meet again. Yes, all these things make the trips up and down the country following one's favourite football team seem worthwhile.

As a counter to the insipid experience of modern living, aesthetic social spacing unlocks doorways to new and exciting adventures. Not only is this type of spacing 'plotted affectively, by the attention guided by *curiosity*[5] and the search for experiential intensity' (Bauman, 1993: 146), but also, and in stark contrast to the objects of cognitive spacing, humans derive the greatest amount of pleasure from those objects with which they are the least familiar. Waxing lyrical about his excursions into more extraordinary landscapes, one supporter eloquently captured the love affair which exists between some travelling supporters and the unfamiliar:

Nick: When you hit a coast, particularly that trip to Plymouth, when you go right along, where you almost feel like the train is in the sea. You know? You've got all these quaint little fishing villages and stuff ... I love that.

Similarly, Eileen described the enjoyment which she derived from visiting Catherine of Aragon's grave during an away day at Peterborough. The village of Yarm (complete with cobbled streets), a well-known stop-off-point for supporters travelling towards Middlesbrough's Riverside stadium, was also singled out by Graham as an example of a 'beautiful' location.

The quest for unfamiliar experiences is not limited to the search for beautiful, cobbled streets and quaint little fishing villages, the unique aesthetic properties of specific football stadiums also constitute an attraction for some supporters. Richard recalled how 'completely awe struck' he was during his first visit to Arsenal's former Highbury stadium, attributing this to both the scale of the noise and sound, and 'just how different it was'. Warren also reflected fondly on his visit to this ground, describing it as 'unique'. 'Sid', in one particularly nostalgic and powerful passage of conversation, even went so far as to describe Arsenal's relocation to another ground as 'unforgivable', claiming that he 'could have wept when they closed it down'. In keeping with the remainder of his 'authenticity' narrative, Sid suggested that both the history and 'superb' design of this stadium (it contained two art-deco stands), meant that it should be thought of as a 'proper ground'.

These novel experiences can help supporters to maintain their enthusiasm for 'away days', thereby facilitating the *moral* desire to stay loyal and to use Richard's expression, 'represent' the club. However, two key threats to these supporters' quest for novelty can be identified. The first of these is the outcome of a concerted effort by the British Police force to diffuse any potential conflict within and around English football stadiums by 'shepherding' supporters into pre-allocated hostelries. The second is posed by the modernisation of English football grounds.

A key weapon in the police force's fight against football hooliganism is their right to restrict the movements of supporters who they consider to be potentially troublesome (see Pearson and James, 2015). This practice has a direct impact on travelling football supporters, whether hooligan or otherwise, due to the propensity to treat these two groups as one and the same. One strategy which is used to help maintain law and order is the 'shepherding' of travelling football supporters into pre-allocated public houses. Customarily this involves explaining to supporters where they can and cannot go when they arrive in the municipality of the home team. This practice which curtails the pursuit of aesthetic thrills, including the search for novelty, is both contentious and considered in some quarters as archaic:

Craig: I completely and utterly hate it ... I don't see in this day and age, the police can tell you what you can and can't do, on a liberty of, 'Can I walk down that street or can I walk down that street, can I come off the train station on that entrance or are you telling me I've got to go on a bus somewhere?'.

Given the value which travelling football supporters attach to the pursuit of novel (new journeys, new towns, new pubs) aesthetic experiences, it should come as little surprise to hear that some have taken measures to circumnavigate these 'restrictive' policing practices. These included hanging around innocuously in train stations until the police had escorted the main body of the travelling contingent into a different location and travelling by minibuses (sometimes along A roads). The presence of a female companion also helped some supporters to convince the police that their intentions were honourable.

The modernisation of English football grounds also poses a threat to the experiential intensity and novelty which travelling football supporters seek. Although a small number welcomed these developments, not least because of their enhanced sense of safety, others are critical of the flat one-dimensional experience which these engender – a physical manifestation of football's desire for amnesia and discontinuity.

Concluding Remark

The post-1989 modernisation of English football presents a threat to the outlook of 'traditional' travelling football supporters. These supporters have sought to resist these developments and manage social space within and around English football stadiums via three 'interwoven, yet distinct' processes (Bauman, 1993: 145). However, the struggle they engage in is an uphill one. It may be the case that the human imagination can help to foster the 'ideal' social space, but something has been lost which cannot be regained. All that remains are the residues of a formerly dominant, but now 'actively residual' – 'alternative or even oppositional' (Williams, 1977: 122) – football culture.

More broadly, my research indicates that the management of football-related social space is a complex phenomenon, which requires its instigators to negotiate three competing imperatives. In keeping with Bauman's conceptualisation, **cognitive** spacing – which functions as a form of knowledge control – can be disturbed by the instinctual **moral** urges and felt sense of responsibility towards others which individuals experience. In the case of football supporters, this might mean abandoning a sense of loyalty to the group to protect the rights of stewards, catering staff, and even police officers. In turn, **aesthetic** spacing can override these moral concerns, the desire for experiential intensity and amusement taking precedence. Regardless, and what this research has demonstrated, is that the relationship between social spacing and control is a complex phenomenon that requires a nuanced explanation. Mindfulness of this can help to avoid over-simplistic analyses of the relationship between domination and resistance.

Notes

1 Sections of this chapter first published in Woolsey, I (2021) *Football Fans and Social Spacing: Power and Control in a Modernising Landscape*. Cham. Palgrave Macmillan.
2 A Sheffield Theatre.
3 My brackets.
4 My emphasis.
5 My emphasis.

References

Adorno, T, Frenkel-Brunswik, E, Levinson, D, & Nevitt Sandord, R (1950) *The Authoritarian Personality*. New York. Harper and Row.
Bauman, Z (1993) *Postmodern Ethics*. Oxford. Blackwell Publishing.
Bauman, Z (1995) *Life in Fragments*. Oxford. Blackwell Publishers Limited.
Bauman, Z (2001a) *Community: Seeking Safety in an Insecure World*. Cambridge. Polity Press.
Bauman, Z (2001b) *The Individualized Society*. Cambridge. Polity Press.
Beynon, J (2002) *Masculinities and Culture*. Buckingham. Open University Press.

Blackshaw, T (2003) *Leisure Life: Myth, Masculinity and Modernity*. London. Routledge.
Blackshaw, T (2010) *Key Concepts in Community Studies*. London. Sage.
Bramham, P & Wagg, S (2014) *An Introduction to Leisure Studies: Principles and Practice*. London. Sage Publications Ltd.
Conn, D (1997) *The Football Business: Fair Game in the '90s?* Edinburgh. Mainstream Publishing Projects.
Crabbe, T & Brown, A (2004) You're not welcome anymore: The football crowd, class, and social exclusion. In: Wagg, S (eds) *British Football and Social Exclusion*. Oxon. Routledge, pp. 71–81.
Crawford, G (2004) *Consuming Sport: Fans, Sport and Culture*. London. Routledge.
Delanty, G (1999) *Social Theory in a Changing World: Conceptions of Modernity*. Cambridge. Polity Press.
Elias, N & Dunning, E (1986) *Quest for Excitement: Sport and Leisure in the Civilising Process*. Oxford. Blackwell Publishers.
Giulianotti, R (1999) *Football: A Sociology of the Global Game*. Cambridge. Polity Press.
Goodlad, P (23 August 2018) 'Police Scotland fear death from Pyrotechnics in Scottish football'. *BBC Sport*. Available from: https://www.bbc.co.uk/sport/football/45275563.
Huizinga, J (2014) *Homo Ludens: A Study of the Play-Element in Culture*. Mansfield Centre. Martino Publishing.
King, A (1998) *The End of the Terraces: The Transformation of English Football in the 1990s*. London. Leicester University Press.
Langdridge (2007) *Phenomenological Psychology: Theory, Research and Method*. Essex: Pearson Education Limited.
MacDougall, D (1999) Social aesthetics and the Doon School. *Visual Anthropology Review* 15(1), 3–20.
Nietzsche, F (2000) *The Birth of Tragedy*. Oxford. Oxford University Press.
Parry, M & Malcolm D. (2004) England's Barmy army: Commercialization, masculinity and nationalism. *International Review for the Sociology of Sport* 39(1), 75–94.
Pearson, G & James, M (2015) Public order and the rebalancing of football fans' rights: Legal problems with pre-emptive policing strategies and banning orders. *Public Law* 458–475.
Russell, D (1997) *Football and the English*. Preston: Carnegie Publishing Ltd.
Ricoeur, P (1973) Ethics and culture. *Philosophy Today* 17(2), 153–165.
Rojek, C (1995) *Decentring Leisure: Rethinking Leisure Theory*. London. Sage Publications Ltd.
Sandvoss, C (2003) *A Game of Two Halves: Football Television and Globalisation*. London. Routledge.
Schutz, A (1970) *On Phenomenology and Social Relations*. Chicago. The University of Chicago Press.
Schutz, A (1971) *Collected Papers 1: The Problem of Social Reality*. The Hague. Martinus Nijhoff.
Turner, M & Ludvigsen J (2022) Theorizing surveillance and social spacing through football: The fan-opticon and beyond. *Sociology Compass* 17(2), 1–14.
Williams, R (1977) *Marxism and Literature*. Oxford. Oxford University Press.
Woolsey, I (2021) *Football Fans and Social Spacing: Power and Control in a Modernising Landscape*. Cham. Palgrave Macmillan.

4 The Mechanisms of Securitisation, Experiences and Impacts of Social Control, and the Pursuit of Smart Power at the 2022 FIFA World Cup in Qatar

Joel Rookwood

Introduction

Qatar is a sovereign state situated in the Arabian Gulf, which operates as an absolute monarchy under Islamic law. Despite its diminutive scale and population, Qatar is a key member of the Gulf Cooperation Council (GCC). In a contemporary context, Qatar is often associated with its high concentration of abundant gas and oil resources, the exportation of which has enhanced the state's wealth. This has financed extensive state modernisation and investment projects, reshaping Qatar's infrastructure and its regional and global reputation (Giusti and Lamonica, 2023). Despite its lucrative energy sector, the reliance on finite sources which can expose the state to economic shocks has influenced the pursuit of economic diversification. Qatar's response to this challenge has incorporated extensive investment in international sports teams and events (Rookwood, 2019). This was spearheaded particularly by sponsorship agreements with F.C. Barcelona and the acquisition of Paris Saint Germain F.C., together with the successful bid to stage the 2022 FIFA Men's World Cup (WC2022) (Søyland and Moriconi, 2022).

The rationale, approach and impact of such investments have been subject to considerable analysis in political, journalistic and scholarly discourses. Such scrutiny is partly influenced by perceptions of Qatar's lack of sporting culture, achievements and pedigree. Some view these sports-related ventures as attempts to reorientate and differentiate Qatar's image from that of neighbouring states, while challenging broader Orientalist stereotyping. Griffin argues that the latter extends to confronting

> colonial grand narratives long propagated as fact in the Cultural West that continue to perpetuate the stereotype of the Arab as the 'Other', an uncivilized, non-Christian, exotic and inferior entity whose social order exists in diametric opposition to the values and ideas of the West.
> (2019: 1002)

As theoretically contextualised in the following section and articulated throughout this chapter, Qatari investment in sport and particularly football

DOI: 10.4324/9781003453062-4

mega-events (FMEs) has also been framed in relation to the intended but at times problematic use of soft power, envisioned to influence public perception and promote its legitimacy as a sovereign nation-state (Næss, 2023). This has combined with the use of hard power resources, the amalgamation of which has been framed as 'smart power'. Such perspectives and representations have partly been shaped by Qatar's approach to social control and crowd management, notably at WC2022.

The policies underpinning Qatar's investment in global sport and mega-events are shaped by its 2030 National Vision. This reflects a commitment to enhance competitiveness and attract investment, built on human, social, economic and environmental pillars of development. It reveals core challenges, namely how to invest and build sustainably, how to manage migrant labour, and how to modernise the state while preserving traditions. Addressing the latter challenge, Amara and Ishac (2022) analysed the impact of sport mega-events (SMEs) in supporting the model of modern monarchy-states intent on pursuing equilibrium between efficiency (as showcased through mega-event management capacities), and the authenticity of Arab cultural tradition. Recent criticism of Qatari mega-event investments centres on sustainability and legacy issues (Brannagan and Reiche, 2022), the associated demand and long-term usage of infrastructural developments (Næss, 2023), questions of global culture and multiculturalism (Giusti and Lamonica, 2023), the conditions and treatment of migrant workers responsible for such construction (Khalifa, 2020), and the associated social control apparatus in the state (Babar and Vora, 2022). The latter aspect is central to this chapter, extended to mechanisms, experiences and impacts of social control at WC2022.

As my recent work has demonstrated, 'For those seeking to control media narratives and maximise the commercial impact of tournaments, preventing disorder and promoting the positivity of the fan experience have become central to how events are managed and marketed' (Rookwood, 2021: 2). The fan experience has become a pronounced priority across global sport, partly manifest through efforts to engage spectators, providing pre- and post-match entertainment to 'encourage additional interactions, monetised as expenditure and projected through social media engagements' (ibid.: 3). There has also been analysis of 'smart stadium' initiatives intended to enrich the fan experience through improved engagement, convenience, safety, security, sustainability and energy optimisation (Baroncelli and Ruberti, 2022).

This chapter centres on WC2022 but also includes brief insights from two previous competitions in Qatar, the 2011 AFC Asian Cup and 2019 FIFA Club World Cup – and how these experiences may have shaped WC2022. 31 semi-structured interviews were undertaken with international fans across the three events, 17 of which were at WC2022. Respondents were from 16 countries across six continents with all participants having attended at least one major preceding FME. Interviews were conducted at stadiums, fan parks and 'fan village' accommodation. This work identifies some key challenges experienced and lessons learned, which may be useful for Qatar and other event host nations to consider. After outlining the theoretical underpinnings and briefly addressing the context of the three FMEs, this work addresses securitisation at WC2022 and the experiences and perceived impact of social control in Qatar, imbedding short interview extracts throughout.

A Contextualised Theoretical Underpinning: Smart Power and Social Control

The contemporary significance of hosting, investing in and otherwise participating in SMEs is often connected to notions of power and influence, especially in the context of international relations and securitisation. American political scientist Joseph Nye coined the term 'soft power' applied to contexts where the attractiveness of a country's culture, political ideals and policies may prove influential, differentiated from hard power which includes the use of military resources (Nye, 2021). Smart power is framed as a combination of hard and soft variations, both of which can be viewed in dichotomous and continuous terms (see Figure 4.1). Soft power is an established theoretical lens through which modern SMEs are sometimes viewed. Hard power approaches have typically been overlooked or discounted from such perspectives, and yet given the prominence of crowd safety and event security within this space – mechanisms that may fall towards the 'harder' end of the continuum – related apparatus may be relevant here. Rothman's (2011) approach is based on the tools deemed useful for implementing different degrees of soft or hard power, some of which are also worthy of consideration in this context (Figure 4.1).

For states that host SMEs partly to shape media representation while improving their national image, the potential for adverse outcomes has also been articulated (Brannagan and Rookwood, 2016). Such negative consequences have been conceptualised as 'soft disempowerment' in FME contexts, whereby, 'you may upset, offend or alienate others, leading to a loss of attractiveness or influence' whereby, others may be offended or alienated, causing a loss of influence or attractiveness. Such impressions are often shaped by representations conveyed through influential media channels. As an applied example, investment in hosting FMEs can potentially prove detrimental to the

Dichotomous	Hard power (command)		Soft power (co-opt)	
	Coercion	Inducement	Agenda-setting	Attraction
Continuous	Harder powers			Softer powers
Resources	Military	Economic	Institutional	Rhetoric / Success

Figure 4.1 Dichotomous and Continuous Resources and the Continuum of Power (adapted from Rothman, 2011).

intended acquisition of soft power, if associated infrastructural projects are widely associated with human rights violations and the mistreatment of migrant construction workers (Khalifa, 2020), or if collective fan experiences are connected to negative encounters with security apparatus. Such perceptions can bleed into associations with the event itself, and its host nation.

Given the variations and fluidities that may be encompassed within 'the fan experience' alone, such perspectives may not always be clearly defined, neatly categorised, permanently established, or all-encompassing. Therefore, I propose a continuum of soft power and disempowerment here – whereby individuals may perceive or interpret circumstances, events, apparatus and characteristics on sliding scales, perhaps from attractive to offensive. An individual's overall outlook of an FME and its host nation may be formed, but potentially comprising a myriad of micro-impressions which can change over time. Figure 4.2 illustrates a dynamic model simplified here to convey the potential fluidity of soft power applied to particular examples pertinent to this chapter.

The processing of visitors, policing of supporters, management of crowds, prevention of disorder and securitisation of events are established priorities of modern FMEs (Ludvigsen, 2022). Many associated practices have become ingrained, with attending supporters developing experiential frames of reference across contexts. Fans may hold particular expectations and assumptions as a consequence, aspects of which may be shaped by a host nation's cultural environment. Interrelations between fans and police in domestic football may shape respective legislative responses and crowd control practices, some of which have been criticised as disproportionate measures infringing upon civil liberties in certain countries (Pearson and Stott, 2022). When such states host FMEs these concerns can be magnified, particularly when applied to crowds unfamiliar with such social control apparatus (Rookwood, 2022). In some countries, the increasingly legalistic approach to social policy and the rising criminalisation of football fans has seen authorities granted greater powers to arrest and prosecute supporters, with banning orders introduced to prohibit known 'hooligans' from attending matches. This legislative and securitisation framework is applied specifically to football in some cases, differentiated from general sporting contexts.

Some FME organisers have prohibited alcohol consumption due to the perceived risk of violence and the assumed causal link to 'football hooliganism', shaping cultures of distrust. Media coverage of FME disorder reinforces the view of football fans as a threat to be controlled, rather than a

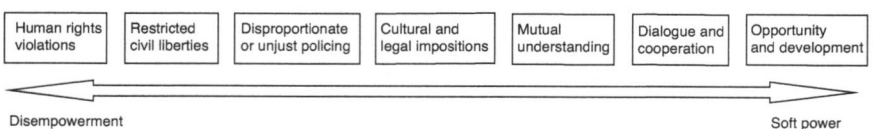

Figure 4.2 A Continuum of Soft (Dis)empowerment.

demographic to be welcomed and an income stream to be capitalised upon (Rookwood, 2021). While partly reframing this perception, the expansion of contemporary FMEs has also complicated the challenge of hosting increasingly large numbers of supporters. Particularly since Germany's 2006 World Cup, many FMEs have featured fan parks in host cities, encouraging broader attendances. These provide facilities for fans to congregate irrespective of allegiances in temporarily erected sites of demarcated but shared spaces, to interact with fans, watch matches on large screens and partake in other forms of entertainment and consumption. These venues have also facilitated event securitisation.

Various interdisciplinary security studies have examined FMEs, focusing on organisational management, policing and legislative analysis. Crowd management theories have typically been informed by sociological, psychological and organisational perspectives. Contemporary theorising views crowd conduct as an often complex, dynamic and unpredictable set of behaviours. Effective FME crowd management often requires approaches considerate of crowd dynamics while appealing to emotional receptiveness through 'dialogue, under-enforcement and negotiation' through dialogue and negotiation. Security personnel at FMEs may find the composite identities, collective behaviours, lived experiences and interpretations of visiting fans may differ from other events, as suggested in advance of WC2022 (see Rookwood, 2019). Procedural Justice Theory suggests that public compliance with the law is best achieved when security personnel demonstrate actions perceived to be legitimate, proportionate and equitable (O'Brien and Tyler, 2019). The connection and potential friction between perceptions of hard power resources and the perceived legitimacy of security approaches is central to this chapter. This multi-layered research is positioned at this theoretical intersection of smart power and social control.

FMEs in Qatar

On 2 December 2010 Russia was declared hosts of the 2018 World Cup, a country almost fifteen-hundred times the size of Qatar. On the same day FIFA announced that Qatar would host WC2022. This proved a momentous statement of power for Qatar, but the associated FIFA scandals and allegations of corruption were also considered early indications of soft disempowerment (Brannagan and Reiche, 2022). The following month Qatar staged the Asian Cup for the second time. The spotlight illuminated a lack of infrastructure, and questions over the long-term demand for the facilities required to host FIFA's flagship event, and Qatar's suitability to manage such a large influx of visiting football fans in a concentrated area. The Asian Cup did provide the experience of hosting diverse and rival nations, with both North Korea and South Korea involved and Iraq playing Iran. However, the event was not well attended, particularly by international visitors. The average attendance for Qatar's four matches was 28,935, while 37,174 were at the final. For the remaining 27 matches, the average audience was 9,324, the lowest being 2,022.

Jordanian fans did offer examples of what Cleland and Giulianotti (2023) term 'carnivalesque' behaviours. As one fan perceptibly argued:

> Jordan fans seemed the most similar to Europeans and South Americans … You could see the security get a bit nervous around them though. They're obviously not used to it, unsure when to intervene … Qatar will either have to train its police force, or just buy in security for the World Cup.
>
> (Fan 3, 12.01.11)

According to Brannagan and Rookwood's (2016) media analysis, the intervening period saw soft disempowerment principally played out on four levels: ongoing allegations of bribery and corruption regarding the acquisition of WC2022; scrutiny of Qatar's human rights record and the conditions imposed upon its migrant workforce; concerns over the health, safety and treatment of players and fans (particularly regarding Qatar's climate and perceived lack of freedom for women and homosexuals); and the likely restriction or even prohibition of alcohol consumption. Interviewees emphasised Qatar's inexperience with hosting '… passionate and rowdy fans in large numbers from different countries … who want to drink alcohol' (Fan 5, 14.01.11).

Qatar subsequently staged consecutive FIFA Club World Cups (FCWC) in 2019 and 2020. Although the scale of these events and the dynamic of support did not compare to a World Cup, they provided useful tests of infrastructural developments and Qatar's preparedness to host WC2022. With respect to the latter, the Hamad International Airport opened in 2014 (awarded the world's best in 2021), and a 37-station, 76-kilometre-long metro network followed in 2019. There were 35,000 hotel beds by 2019, the majority catering for higher classes. However, as infrastructure developed, environmental, ethical and security questions followed. These FCWC events saw enhanced international media criticism of migrant worker conditions and the treatment of certain demographics. There were long post-match queues for metros, as lines of communication and organisation were criticised. However, an open-air fan park was organised at the 2019 FCWC, where alcohol was sold – a first for Qatar, a state which prohibits such consumption under Islamic law. Qatar's Secretary General of the Supreme Committee for Delivery and Legacy Hassan al-Thawadi declared: 'Alcohol is not part of our culture, but hospitality is' (France 24, 2021). One fan considered the fan park to be, '… an authentic fan event … organised by football people for football people. It wasn't a soulless commercial space like most World Cup fan parks. It was organic' (Fan 12, 22.12.19). Another described the security at the event as '… firm but fair' (Fan 7, 18.12.19). Demonstrating the fluidity of Rothman's (2011) model, such positive interviewee impressions of soft power were sometimes mirrored by supportive references to 'harder' mechanisms, namely effective management and control. While it emphasised the importance of professional and cultural networks and partnerships, the Doha fan park also saw no reported alcohol-related incidents or arrests (Rookwood, 2021).

A more pressing security issue for Qatar concerned the GCC diplomatic crisis which was at its midway point in 2019 (Kapar and Buigut, 2020). This temporary cessation of relations between Qatar and various states in the region proved complicated for Qataris but challenging too for Westerners attempting to navigate geographical spaces and political narratives. It made travel in the region difficult for the 2019 and 2020 events, particularly for South American fans – whose qualification is only confirmed a month before the tournament, giving less time to secure bookings. Regional relations had stabilised by January 2021, with the build-up to WC2022 largely dominated instead by the COVID-19 pandemic. Writing in early 2021, I proposed that SMEs in this era modelled on attracting international visitors relied upon freedom of movement and open borders, while necessitating 'a thus far elusive internationally-coordinated containment and vaccination programme to accelerate the advent of a post-pandemic era' (Rookwood, 2021: 16).

The delayed Tokyo Olympics and Euro 2020 staged between June and August 2021 provided observers – including Qatar's World Cup Supreme Committee for Delivery and Legacy – with key lessons for staging COVID-secure sporting events (Rookwood and Adeosun, 2021). By November 2022, global COVID-19 case were declining, and vaccine programmes were widely established, with the timing of WC2022 helping provide what one interviewee called 'a fresh start for global sport' (Fan 21, 25.11.22), echoing Al-Thani et al. (2022). However, with Euro 2020 staged across 11 countries, there were stark differences evident in COVID-19 measures as well as crowd dynamics and social control. The disorder at the Wembley final in particular (which followed violence at the 2016 event), was a reminder of the potential security challenges facing subsequent event organisers, including WC2022.

Mechanisms of Securitisation

> For modern major events, especially the World Cup and Olympics, event security begins well in advance of the tournament. The threat of terrorism, fan disorder, global health, a diplomatic crisis, these issues put hosts in the spotlight. The media coverage sees to that ... Qatar's [World Cup] has been controversial from day one ... Bringing so many fans together in such a small space, the security is complicated (Fan 17, 20.11.22).

A key issue facing World Cup security operations concerns the access, processing and identification of international attendees (Rookwood, 2021). The 2018 World Cup pioneered a multipurpose visa and identification system termed Fan I.D. This physical document enabled 1.5 million fans including 630,000 international spectators from over 100 countries to visit Russia during the event, with cards required for immigration control, stadium access and free city transport. This provided precedent for Qatar's Hayya Card system, which adopted a digital format for WC2022, as with the majority of match tickets.

Incorporating identity cards for football matches had long been resisted as a draconian measure in some countries, but according to one interviewee, 'There is general acceptance of fan identification cards now, for security' (Fan 23, 25.11.22). However, this system did incur logistical and technological challenges. Some WC2022 games had empty seats, partly because spare tickets were not easily transferable. The electronic access systems that are becoming established practice were unfamiliar for some and relied upon internet connectivity as well as mobile devices. As one fan noted: 'Some people have had issues with phones dying and internet connections at stadiums … You have to download the Hayya app on arrival, which allows Qataris to track your movements and access your data' (Fan 22, 24.11.22). Similar concerns were expressed by news agencies, some of whom labelled the app as 'spyware' (Manacourt, 2022).

After being awarded WC2022, the state of Qatar sought to enhance its security capabilities and policing practices. In 2012, Interpol established Project Stadia, a decade-long initiative partly funded by Qatar, initiated to support countries intent on hosting SMEs. This created a Centre of Excellence and developed networks of security experts. Training programmes included crisis management, behaviour analysis, maintaining safety and public order at sports events, and fighting hate crimes. Qatar formulated a WC2022 security strategy, operationalised on logistical, human and technical levels. A Security and Safety Operations Committee was established, which executed various plans, training courses, programmes and joint exercises to enhance government and private security capabilities and better integrate the roles of civil and military entities. This included designing and implementing the Sports Crowd Security and Safety Programme, and others focusing on crowd management, human rights, first aid, crowd cooperations, traffic management and facility evacuation simulations. A total of 49,000 government and private personnel participated in these programmes. Various exercises, security simulations and readiness tests were undertaken, namely the Watan Exercise in November 2021 and the Last Mile Security Conference in May 2022. The latter involved contributions from liaison officers from the International Police Coordination Centre, which was first activated at Qatar's 2019 FCWC. Participating parties extended to countries who had qualified for WC2022. This was intended to solidify coordination and facilitate information exchange between Qatar, Interpol and representatives of various international police services.

Numerous security agreements and memorandums of understanding and cooperation were signed with countries containing specialised forces, who approved the provision of support in securitising the event were it to be required. Such agreements were partly intended to foster cooperation with specialised European police and Europol experts, and the International Centre for Sports

into being in the heart of Europe, in the heart of the most beautiful mountainous land in the world." The scientific perspective of the authors of the initiative was obvious. At one point, they even described their project as a "great experiment to restore primordial alpine nature and, at the same time, to bequeath to the future a major refuge of pristine natural life."[15]

Preserving evidence of the past from eclipse enjoyed a boom in those years of rapid societal change that was reflected in simultaneous efforts in archeology and ethnology, in conservation of monuments and heritage, as well as in the creation and expansion of museums.[16] The SNK's intention to restore primordial nature was also in keeping with the times. Even within cultural heritage and art history, debates were raging over the extent to which restoration of all buildings and works of art could return them to their "original" condition.[17] The general popularity and familiarity of such concerns smoothed the way for the SNK. On the other hand, Paul Sarasin and his colleagues skillfully exploited the resulting opportunities to gain allies and to strengthen their own position.

Thus, the "reserve question" was not only pursued by the SNK but was also taken up, in parallel, by the Swiss Forest Association (*Schweizerischer Forstverein*) and the Swiss Heritage Society (*Schweizerische Vereinigung für Heimatschutz*). The latter organization, which had only just been founded in 1905, like the SNK first had to establish a profile that would permit it to take stands on issues and to develop positions. The former, the forest association, had begun to tackle the establishment of "primordial forest reserves" at the suggestion of one of its members, Robert Glutz, in 1906. The foresters, too, were primarily interested in scientific studies of the natural development of nature—in this case, forests—in areas exempt from land use. The SNK and the forestry association subsequently exchanged ideas and plans on a regular basis, but continued to work separately on their own projects. By 1911, the forestry association had established three small "primordial forest reserves" ranging between five and forty hectares, or twelve and ninety-nine acres. After the founding of the national park in the Engadine, one-third of whose area was covered by forest, interest in individual forest reserves dwindled perceptibly, so much so that in 1919 the association shut down its own three reserves.[18]

The SNK managed very neatly to secure the support of the national government. In August 1907, the Federal Council independently approached the SNG with the request that it review a petition the council had received from the *Société de Physique et d'Histoire naturelle de Genève* for "geological and geographic reserves" modeled on the American national parks. The motivation for the petition was a controversy sparked some months earlier by the application of a license for a railway to the top of the Matterhorn. The action unleashed a storm of protest that drew attention to cultural heritage through the organization of a national petition. The SNK also seized the opportunity, but did not join the protest movement owing to internal differences of opinion.[19] The Geneva scientific society now proposed classifying the Matterhorn as a "reserve," which of course threw the railway plans into disarray. Federal Councilor Josef Zemp, who as head of the railway department had received the letter, forwarded it to his colleague Mark-Emile Ruchet in the Department of Home Affairs with the recommendation that he seriously consider the proposal: "No doubt, this idea is not new, and Switzerland could long ago have taken a page from the United States and created national reserves in different areas that would have lacked neither utility nor renown. If it was not done, it is surely because we believed that vast regions of our Alps would remain intact and would constitute natural and desirable reserves without any state intervention whatsoever. Today, we must acknowledge that such is not the case. The push of the railways is sparing no part of the land, and the 'entrapment' of our most beautiful peaks is proceeding apace."[20] Ruchet referred the matter to the SNG and its chair, Fritz Sarasin, a move that clearly reflected management practices at the time. Since the small federal administration lacked knowledge and manpower, it routinely relied on the expertise of professional societies. Sarasin accepted the job with alacrity, and in this way was able to integrate the federal councilor advantageously into his own network.[21]

The controversy surrounding the Matterhorn continued to smolder up to the First World War, when the war-related slump in the tourism sector showed that implementation of the project might be illusory. Although the SNK refrained from intervening in further developments, the public debate over Swiss mountain scenery made it easier for the SNK to convince both the authorities and the public of the urgency of conservation. In five years, if urgent steps were not taken, "the most beautiful parts of Switzerland would be criss-crossed with hotel blocks and railroad tracks," opined Hermann Christ in May 1908 in the Basel newspaper. As a countermeasure, Christ recommended establishing "Swiss national parks." As with Federal Councilor Zemp, for Christ the Matterhorn plans symbolized the omnipotence of modern technology, which even the hitherto forbidding alpine peaks were now helpless against. Their preservation had to be addressed with the utmost urgency. Christ himself wrote: "It is high time, the eleventh hour. Let us make haste to accomplish as least the essential steps before the Matterhorn vandalism is a *fait accompli*."[22]

Laying the Foundations

At the end of August 1908, the members of the SNK gathered in Glarus for their yearly meeting. The main item on the agenda was the presentation and discussion of the results of the national survey on future reserves. The proposal for the Ofengebiet clearly stood out. In addition to the report on Val Cluozza, Brunies, who had been invited to the meeting, read out a letter from the com-

instances of crowd disorder in Qatar were sporadic and limited. Reflecting on the first week of WC2022, another interviewee noted:

> There have been a few issues with Latin American fans, Mexico and Argentina especially, but generally speaking, those who've come haven't presented a challenge to the police ... Fan violence at Euro 2016 was much worse. It's partly where an event is and the kinds of fans it attracts, which creates the security challenge.
> (Fan 22, 24.11.22)

There was a fan festival and three fan village cabin sites at WC2022. The fan villages were considered to be,

> Quite isolated. The only fans there were staying at them. They had big screens showing matches, and enough security ... The fan parks only served alcohol at set times, and the security seemed pretty effective. The hotels serving alcohol had their own security.
> (Fan 20, 24.11.22)

In the build up to WC2022, alcohol consumption proved a prevalent concern regarding social control, which was permitted in hotels and fan parks at certain times and spaces, but not at stadiums. One respondent argued: 'Most events where alcohol is banned, it's because of fan violence. That doesn't say much for the host's ability to manage fans and treat them with respect' (Fan 23, 25.11.22). However, the same interviewee added:

> But in Qatar it was a separate issue. It was about respecting their culture. Even fans who wanted to drink seemed to respect the reason they weren't allowed to. Some fans felt it was a safer and more inclusive space as a result too.
> (ibid.)

For those who travelled, WC2022 may partly be remembered for Qatar's policy on alcohol consumption, which ultimately represented a statement of power as well as a degree of compromise without cultural concession. For some, this dynamic altered and perhaps enhanced the atmosphere and fan experience.

Finally, there were very few reported incidents of criminality at WC2022. It could be argued that this reflects a generally effective security operation. However, one example during the opening week of the tournament was well publicised, less so for the details of the robbery than the subsequent response it illuminated. An Argentine reporter had her bag stolen while she was broadcasting live from the Doha fan zone. Qatari authorities asked her whether she would like the criminal to be deported or imprisoned for five years. As one fan argued: 'AI would have caught the criminal, and anyone else found breaking the law. You can't escape it here' (Fan 20, 24.11.22). Qatar set up a technology hub at the Aspire Command and Control Centre to monitor fans at venues and on public transport. With experts from cybersecurity, anti-terrorism and transportation, over 100 technicians closely monitored images on screens via 200,000 units, from 22,000 security cameras. Facial recognition technology enabled the crew to zoom in on individuals. The Centre's director Hamad Ahmed al-Mohannadi stated: 'With one click you can shift from one stadium to [another] stadium, because we have everything integrated through our centralised platform, in terms of facility management, security, health and safety, and ICT operations'. One fan reflected:

> Some say AI security makes a place safer, that if you don't break the law then it shouldn't bother you. But it gives the impression of a police state, giving the state powers they can easily abuse ... With AI we're just at the beginning.
>
> (Fan 17, 20.11.22)

Conclusion

This research demonstrates a significant but at times overlooked aspect of Qatar's mega-event legacies. Hosting events across different periods has facilitated the development of the state's approach to security and control over time. As the pinnacle of their portfolio, staging WC2022 provided unprecedented opportunities for Qatar to enhance their domestic security expertise through training programmes, joint exercises, and knowledge transfer, while improving security protocols and policing practices. The lack of serious security issues and instances of criminality during the event could be perceived to demonstrate the effectiveness of the integrated security operation, involving the processing of visitors, and monitoring, policing and managing crowds. Qatar's event was a welcome re-start for global SMEs in a post-COVID context, set among newly normalised relations in the GCC. Although WC2022 and Qatar's other sporting and SME investments are shaped by its 2030 National Vision – sometimes seen through the lens of soft power – the necessity of incorporating hard power mechanisms to securitise the event has yielded a combined approach that might be framed as smart power.

The majority of those who follow globally significant SMEs currently do so remotely, through the lens of broadcasters and social media platforms. Those who attend in person may develop different perspectives of host nations. An individual's overall outlook may comprise a myriad of micro-impressions. Collective memory of Qatar and WC2022 may be shaped by Argentina's victory and Lionel Messi's crowning glory. Others may emphasise the various corruption charges and human rights violations, despite Qatar's labour reforms and improvements to migrant worker conditions (Brannangan and Ryche, 2022). Given the potential fluidities of soft power, cognitive detachment may take time. Constructing eight stadiums with a combined 390,090 capacity within a fifty-mile radius in a country with 313,000 citizens and a 2.9 million mostly migrant population with limited sporting pedigree will inevitably incur criticism. And yet, in seeking to apply the lessons learned and use the facilities constructed, Qatar will stage a third Asian Cup in January 2024, bringing their FME journey and this chapter full circle. Total capacities of venues will have almost quadrupled between Asian Cup events, from 108,403 to 402,782. This is 'capacity building' – although the next challenge will be to fill the stadiums, and ensure the security and safety of those who attend.

References

Al-Thani, H, Al Musleh, A A, Khan, N A, Asim, M, Abdurahiman, S, Morad, Y A, Massey, A, & El-Menyar, A (2022) FIFA Arab Cup Tournament with full capacity of spectators during the COVID-19 pandemic: A cross-sectional study. *Science and Medicine in Football* 7(4), 337–346. https://doi.org/10.1080/24733938.2022.2110276

Amara, M & Ishac, W (2022) Sport and development in Qatar. International and regional dynamics of sport mega-events. In: Tinaz, C & Knott, B (eds) *Sport and Development in Emerging Nations*. Abingdon. Routledge, pp. 142–154.

Babar, Z & Vora, N (2022) The 2022 World Cup and migrants' rights in Qatar: Racialised labour hierarchies and the influence of racial capitalism. *The Political Quarterly* 93(3), 498–507. https://doi.org/10.1111/1467-923X.13154

Baroncelli, A & Ruberti, M (2022) Smart sport arenas make cities smarter. In: Visvizi, A & Troisi, O (eds) *Managing Smart Cities*. Cham. Springer, pp. 89–104.

Brannagan, P M & Reiche, D (2022) *Qatar and the 2022 FIFA World Cup: Politics, Controversy, Change*. Cham. Palgrave Macmillan.

Brannagan, P M & Rookwood, J (2016) Sports mega-events, soft power and soft disempowerment: International supporters' perspectives on Qatar's acquisition of the 2022 FIFA World Cup finals. *International Journal of Sport Policy and Politics* 8(2), 173–188. https://doi.org/10.1080/19406940.2016.1150868

Cleland, J & Giulianotti, R (2023) A sociological analysis of United Kingdom football fans: Historical debates and contemporary issues. In: Buarque de Hollanda, B & Busset, T (eds) *Football Fandom in Europe and Latin America*. Cham. Palgrave Macmillan, pp. 37–57.

France 24 (1 February 2021) Alcohol in 2022 World Cup stadiums – For those who can Pay. https://www.france24.com/en/live-news/20210201-alcohol-in-2022-world-cup-stadiums-for-thosewho-can-pay

Giusti, S & Lamonica, A G (2023) The geopolitics of culture: Museum proliferation in Qatar and Abu Dhabi. *The International Spectator*. https://doi.org/10.1080/03932729.2023.2192611

Griffin, T R (2019) National identity, social legacy and Qatar 2022: The cultural ramifications of FIFA's first Arab World Cup. *Soccer & Society* 20(7–8), 1000–1013. https://doi.org/10.1080/14660970.2019.1680499

Kapar, B, & Buigut, S (2020) Effect of Qatar diplomatic and economic isolation on Qatar stock market volatility: An event study approach. *Applied Economics* 52(55), 6022–6030. https://doi.org/10.1080/00036846.2020.1781776

Khalifa, N A-D (2020) Analysis of the impediments to the effective management of mega sporting events: A case of the FIFA 2022 World Cup in Qatar. *European Journal of Business and Strategic Management* 5(1), 70–95.

Ludvigsen, J A (2022) Examining stakeholder outlooks on football policing and security: The case of Euro 2020. *Journal of Sport and Social Issues* 46(4), 363–382. https://doi.org/10.1177/01937235211043650

Manacourt, V (15 November 2022) Don't download Qatar World Cup apps, EU warn. *Politico*. https://www.politico.eu/article/qatar-world-cup-app-data-warning/

Næss, H E (2023) A figurational approach to soft power and sport events: The case of the FIFA World Cup Qatar 2022™. *Frontiers in Sports and Active Living* 6(5), 1142878. https://doi.org/10.3389/fspor.2023.1142878

Nye, J S (2021) Soft power: The evolution of a concept. *Journal of Political Power* 14(1), 196–208. https://doi.org/10.1080/2158379X.2021.1879572

O'Brien, TC, & Tyler, TR (2019). Rebuilding trust between police & communities through procedural justice & reconciliation. *Behavioral Science & Policy*, 5(1), 34–50. https://doi.org/https://doi.org/10.1353/bsp.2019.0003

Pearson, G, & Stott, C (2022) *A New Agenda for Football Crowd Management: Reforming Legal and Policing Responses to Risk*. Cham. Palgrave Macmillan.

Rookwood, J (2019) Access, security and diplomacy: Perceptions of soft power, nation branding and the organisational challenges facing Qatar's 2022 FIFA World Cup. *Sport, Business Management* 9(1), 26–44. https://doi.org/10.1108/SBM-02-2018-0016

Rookwood, J (2021) Diversifying the fan experience and securitising crowd management: A longitudinal analysis of fan park facilities at 15 football mega events between 2002 and 2019. *Managing Sport and Leisure*. https://doi.org/10.1080/23750472.2021.1985596

Rookwood, J (2022) From sport-for-development to sports mega-events: Conflict, authoritarian modernisation and statecraft in Azerbaijan. *Sport in Society* 25(4), 847–866. https://doi.org/10.1080/17430437.2021.2019710

Rookwood, J & Hoey, P (2024) From the anfield wrap to boss night and the paris protests: Football, politics, identity and the cultural evolution of fan media and supporter activism in liverpool. *International Journal of the Sociology of Leisure* 7, 83–107.

Rothman, S B (2011) Revising the soft power concept: What are the means and mechanisms of soft power? *Journal of Political Power* 4(1), 49–64. https://doi.org/10.1080/2158379X.2011.556346

Søyland, H S & Moriconi, M (2022) Qatar's multi-actors sports strategy: Diplomacy, critics and legitimisation. *International Area Studies Review* 25(4), 354–374. https://doi.org/10.1177/22338659221120065

Wu, X (2023) A study of differences in media coverage of news reports-an example of Iranian players' refusal to sing the national anthem during the 2022 World Cup. *Journal of Education, Humanities and Social Sciences* 13, 232–238. https://doi.org/10.54097/ehss.v13i.7899

rights of the park spaces for ninety-nine years, for which it would pay their owners the yearly sum of up to 30,000 francs. In the National Council, which was the first of the two legislative chambers to deal with the proposal, a protracted debate ensued again but resulted in no substantial changes. Criticism came from the ranks of the council's leftist members. Whereas a few members of the socialist faction would have preferred to use the federal money for social purposes than for nature conservation, a group led by Glarner democrat David Legler fought against the project on principle. Legler considered the information on the extinction of animal and plant species to be highly exaggerated and for that reason denied the need for a large reserve. The biggest beneficiaries of the national park would be predators, whose protection Legler described not only as an "absurdity" but also a threat to visitors to the park and the surrounding areas. That no large predators inhabited the park weakened Legler's argument. In any event, the possibility of intervention was included in the case bears did return—which proponents hoped would happen—or some other undesirable development came to pass. Article 1 of the resolution was amended to state that "all flora and fauna is allowed to develop naturally and protected from any human influence *that is not consistent with the goals of the national park.*"[41] In this way, the concerns of some of the parliamentarians were addressed.

In criticizing another aspect of the project, Legler touched a sore spot: If you really want to set up a national park, he argued in the National Council, then put it right in the middle of the Swiss Alps, where it can benefit the Swiss and be properly monitored. Neither of these requirements was guaranteed at the proposed site at the Swiss-Italian border. Consequently, the park would primarily be a "rich hunting ground" for Italian poachers. In fact, in the following years, attacks from the Italian side did become a major worry for the park administration. Moreover, with the nationalization of the park, the question of national representativeness took on significant weight. A member of the Council of States confessed that he did not really understand "what was so Swiss about a high forest in the Engadine. All our neighboring states, Austria, Bavaria, Württemberg, will always have forests that are much more beautiful and rich in wildlife than we Swiss, so we will not be creating anything of specific national interest."[42] In fact, in the wake of this criticism, the criteria for selecting the area began to shift: Scientific justification began to give way to categories related to national policy. In 1910, Carl Schröter was already requesting that "the most characteristic example of each type of pristine nature worthy of preservation be delivered untouched and sacrosanct to posterity." The "alpine national park in the Lower Engadine" would be a first step.[43] When, during the interwar period, the establishment of further national parks was considered, even scientists weighed the question of location no longer on environmental grounds but on political representation. The hosts of the next two national parks should not be the Mittelland (midlands) and Jura—the other two major geographical areas of Switzerland—but French-speaking western Switzerland and Italian-speaking Ticino. Accordingly, in the 1920s plans were introduced for a "Swiss French national park" in the area of Haut de Cry in Valais and a "Swiss Italian national park" around Castagnola-Gandria. Both, however, soon foundered.[44]

Coming into effect as it did on 1 August 1914, the Swiss national day, the federal resolution decreeing a national park in the Lower Engadine was symbolically freighted. However, the coincidence was not the result of careful planning but rather the expiration in mid-July of the three-month deadline for the referendum mandating the measure. All the same, the symbolism of the date was certainly fortuitous for the participants. In its annual report, the SNK called the park "our national nature sanctuary."[45] There was no official ceremony, possibly because the park had de facto already been long established, but also perhaps because international tensions had peaked in recent weeks and the start of the war prevented the relevant preparations. When, in the following months, the First World War drove a wedge between German- and French-speaking Switzerland, and people on both sides sympathized openly with their respective linguistic community, the SNG urged national unity. In 1916, the SNG held its annual meeting in Scuol, on the edge of the national park, and the traditional excursion naturally led through it. In a speech from Alp Mingèr, Carl Schröter praised the park as "a reflection of the true cooperation of all confederates: situated at the extreme eastern limit of our country, in the area of *alt fry Rätia* [old, free Raetia] among our valiant Romansh, from Schanf to Scuol, it is enthusiastically supported by western Switzerland. ... Thus, the park is a work of joint national dedication, a symbol of unity, the most idealistic form of centralization." Before the excursion continued, the national anthem was sung. During a subsequent break, Paul Sarasin gave a speech in French in which he stressed the overall character of the national park.[46] All the well-intentioned rhetoric could not, however, disguise the fact that the park was not only geographically distant from French-speaking Switzerland. In Romandy it was perceived as a Swiss-German institution. That it was located in the Romansh-speaking (and not the German-speaking) part of the country did nothing to dispel this perception since at the time the Romansh were viewed not as a distinct national minority but were counted among the Swiss-German majority. In 1920, to counteract the Germanic influence, the ENPK was expanded to include an additional French-speaking member. As in the Swiss executive, the Federal Council, henceforth two of the seven park commission members would be French speaking. In so doing, at least at the federal government level the national park conformed to the delicate realities of Swiss representation.[47]

back to the sixteenth century where drinking places such as pubs and ales houses were central to the leisure activities of both working and aristocracy classes. Nevertheless, during the late 1800s and early 1900s with the banning of cruel sporting activities and the development of new sports such as the two most widespread codes of football (association and rugby), the alcohol industry became ancillary to sport by occupying a secondary but nonetheless important position in terms of its cultural consumption (Collins and Vamplew, 2002; Mason, 1980; P Dixon and Garnham, 2005). As Vamplew (2016) argued, the *sporting product* of attending live football games in stadium were never offered as a stand-alone good but was incorporated and packaged together with other services such as betting and alcohol consumption. In a way, the alcohol industry exploited the historical cultural consumption links with sport by further associating itself through important advertising activities that further sedimented it as an important facet in terms of what it means to *consume sport* (McCrae, 2008; Jackson, 2014; Cody and Jackson, 2016). While it is possible to argue that those close connections are better encapsulated by British football culture in terms of its longstanding cultural association with pubs, where they are considered as integral spaces for supporting practices (K Dixon, 2014; Petersen-Wagner, 2017b; 2017c), the links between spectating sport and alcohol have worldwide reach (Nicholson et al., 2014; Thompson et al., 2011; Cody and Jackson, 2016).

However, those historical links are not without controversies. Scholars have long debated if alcohol sponsorship and advertisement in sport have potential negative effects on athletes and supporters alike. It is important to note as Gee et al. (2017) do that alcohol-related involvement in spectating sport goes beyond traditional commercial break advertisement but encompasses multiple different promotional images that are accessible to millions worldwide through television broadcasting. For instance, Gee et al. (2017) show how during the broadcasting of major international sporting events camera angles and close ups show crowds consuming alcoholic beverages which has the potential to frame how individuals and groups understand what it means to spectate a live sporting event. While some of the images during broadcasting focus on health-related messages in terms of responsible drinking (Gee et al., 2017), evidence show that those types of messages do not have an influence on alcohol consuming behaviours (Kelly et al., 2018). Moreover, as O'Brien and Kypri (2008) have shown, athletes who have alcohol-related sponsors personally or as part of their club are more associated with hazardous and problematic drinking behaviours raising important ethical questions regarding this association. This is also evident when analysing university-level athletes who either personally or as part of their club have sponsorship links with alcohol-related organisations (O'Brien et al., 2014). Those issues led to national, regional, and international legislations regarding alcohol-related sponsorship and advertisement, which are and were important revenue sources for clubs (Cody and Jackson, 2016; Gee et al., 2021). For instance, during the 2014 FIFA Men's World Cup there were 2.76 alcoholic brand appearances per minute during in-game broadcasting, and 0.83 brand appearances per minute during out-of-game broadcasting, which were coupled with persistent violations regarding International Alliance for Responsible Drinking Guiding Principles (Noel et al., 2016). As Vendrame (2016) highlights, in the Brazilian context beer and wine are not legally considered as alcoholic beverages for marketing purposes, therefore the control in terms of audience and message falls into the remit of a non-governmental organisation (Brazilian Advertising Self-Regulation Council – CONAR), meaning that 'in practical terms, the alcohol industry does not encounter significant limitations when defining the content and the target audience' (Vendrame, 2016: 82), which ultimately paves the way for such *violations* encountered by Noel et al. (2016). Moreover, during the 2018 FIFA Men's World Cup unhealthy products such as alcoholic beverages have featured prominently during television broadcasts in the UK being the category with the second most exposure during in-game broadcasting, and the third during out-of-game broadcasting (Ireland et al., 2021).

Furthermore, what those links through advertisement and sponsorship do is to reinforce and promote a hegemonic masculinity group identity that intertwines alcohol consumption and spectating sport (Wenner and Jackson, 2009). As Jackson (2014) highlights, advertising campaigns that couple alcohol, sport, and masculinity become *cultural manuals* in how to enact a certain *desirable* identity, which tends to omit other forms of masculinity (Gee and Jackson, 2012). Those *cultural manuals* glorify the holy trinity of sport, masculinity, and alcohol consumption turning into 'stylish and desirable lifestyle' (Messner and Montez de Oca, 2005: 1879) that young men aspire to have. Therefore, this specific hegemonic masculinity identity is reinforced by those sponsorship and advertisement agreements leading to other issues such as underage drinking (Davies, 2009) and violent behaviour (Gee, 2014).

As Palmer and Thompson (2007) show, alcohol consumption is an inherent aspect of the cultural consumption of being a sport fan that has ramifications into violent behaviour. While Palmer and Thompson (2007) do not explicitly conceptualise the 'in yer face' behaviour as violent per se, the descriptions provided by the authors amount to symbolic violence in terms of homophobic and misogynistic comments and songs. More recently, as Bandura et al. (2023) argue the *carnivalesque* atmosphere by football crowds is anchored on a collective habitus in which alcohol consumption is integral to the cultural consumption of going to football stadium, nevertheless this alcohol-based behaviour is being replaced by one that is grounded on the use of illegal drugs such as cocaine. In their view (ibid.), fans physical violent behaviour is now more connected to the use of illegal drugs than to the consumption of alcohol. In a similar fashion, Purves et al. (2022) argue that while fans see alcohol as an important facet in the cultural fabric of supporting their club, they do not perceive its consumption as being the cause of physically violent behaviour. This is particular true for younger fans who have not experienced crowd violence stemming from alcohol consumption in contrast to their older counterparts, therefore having a more positive view on alcohol (ibid.). Furthermore, the way in which media frames physically violent crowd behaviour by associating it with the consumption of alcohol (Cleland and Cashmore, 2016) might create a sense of moral panic (Gee, 2014) that contributes to different views on the associations between alcohol and violence. Nonetheless, as dos Reis (2012) show in her analysis, alcohol consumption and abuse were a driver for the legislation in Brazil regarding controlling crowd violence, even if pointing it as sole root and cause would be an 'unacceptable reductionism' (dos Reis, 2012: 80).

In sum, while alcohol consumption is historically tied to sport spectating to a point in which it becomes an inherent aspect of the cultural consumption of sport, its role, prominence, and the perceptions of its association with deviant behaviour such as crowd physical and symbolic violence has mutated over the years. Hence, as a cultural element it becomes a reflection of wider trends in society, and therefore how groups and individuals incorporate it into their habitus.

Methods

As Luhmann (2000: 1) argues 'whatever we know about our society, or indeed about the world we live, we know through the mass media', presupposing that the way media frames stories – either consciously or unconsciously – has the power to influence audiences' perceptions of topics (Scheufele, 1999). As Foucault (1969) argues, discourses, being them written or pictorial, construct 'reality' and in its turn this same 'reality' frames discourses in a dialectical fashion. Therefore, when journalists and editors decide which content to focus on and how to present it for its audience, they are *constructing* a reality, particularly when this reality is unfamiliar to that audience (Graber, 1989). Moreover, as Gamson (1989) argues factual news have no intrinsic meaning unless they are given meaning by being embedded in frames and storylines that help audiences to make sense of them. In a way, those frames act as reference points (*frames of references*) to which audiences are familiar with in their daily lives (Goffman, 1986). According to Entman (1993) framing involves two important aspects, being them the selection of news – what will feature or not – and the salience given to news in terms of space – number of words and position – in a particular medium such as a newspaper. Moreover, framing works by defining problems, diagnosing its causes, making moral judgements, and finally suggesting solutions to those problems (Entman, 1993). In this regard, framing operates in accordance with other media effects theory such as priming and agenda setting (Weaver, 2007; Tewksbury and Scheufele, 2020) in such a way that it is possible to think of news stories in terms of persuasive communication techniques that influence public opinion (Lippmann, 1922).

As such, the chapter analyses how the legalisation of alcohol consumption in stadiums during the 2014 FIFA Men's World Cup in Brazil was framed as *problematic* by the media. To comprehend the wider framing – how alcohol legalisation was situated alongside the staging of the World Cup – I have approached it by focusing on how the *'Lei Geral da Copa'* (General Law of the World Cup) was presented in a particular newspaper. As a federal law that was legislated by the Chamber of Deputies and Senate in Brasília and promulgated by the then President Dilma Roussef in 2012 (Presidência da República, 2012), I have focused the analysis on a newspaper that is produced in the Federal capital. *Correio Braziliense* was the first daily newspaper founded in the new Brazilian capital in April 1960 (Correio Braziliense, 2020) – the day that the capital was inaugurated after its construction – and currently is one of the daily newspapers in Brazil with the highest circulation figures (Statista, 2021). By using the *Biblioteca Nacional* digital archive (Biblioteca Digital Nacional, 2023) and searching for 'Lei Geral da Copa' between 2010 and 2019 on this specific newspaper, I have found 286 matches on 255 different pages. Those stories went through frame analysis following Entman's (1993) four stages functions, considering that not all stages might be present on each story. As aforementioned, the particular focus here on this chapter was on how alcohol legalisation was defined as a *problem* by the media, and what were the frames used by media to *persuade* audiences to construct this viewpoint.

Results and Discussion

As Eick (2010: 279) points out 'every four years and for a time period of four weeks, FIFA invades cities, beforehand setting rules and regulations the applicants for holding the event have to obey to – including but not limited to infrastructure demands, advertisement regulations, safety and security rules' which in the case of the FIFA 2014 Men's World Cup was legislated via the *'Lei Geral da Copa'* (Presidência da República, 2012). Between the different regulations contained in the law, it covered from intellectual property and commercial activities, restrictive areas, image and audio capture and broadcasting, civil and penal sanctions, visa and work permits, ticket sales with concession prices for students, over 60s, and participants in programmes of income transfer (e.g., *Bolsa Família*), to more permanent dispositions as prizes to former Brazilian footballers who have won the 1958, 1962 and 1970 FIFA Men's World Cup (there were no prizes for 1994 World Cup winners). While there were no formal mentions to the legalisation of alcohol commercialisation and consumption within FIFA areas – a 2km radius around stadiums – Article 11 stipulates that FIFA and *individuals* indicated by them have exclusivity in promoting, distributing, selling, and publicising their brands. This article opened the possibility for FIFA partners such as AB InBev's (the Belgian-Brazilian mega-conglomerate) popular brand Budweiser to exclusively commercialise beer within that radius. The *legalisations* of alcohol consumption in stadiums during the 2013 Confederations Cup and 2014 World Cup then became a central point in media debates because of the *prohibition*[1] coming from the *Estatuto do Torcedor* legislation (Presidência da República, 2003).[2] The analysis revealed three main frames that *Correio Braziliense* used to portray the debate surrounding the legalisation of alcohol commercialisation and consumption in football stadiums during the tournaments organised by FIFA in Brazil.

Initially, *Correio Braziliense* sought to frame the legalisation as another polemical point within the *Lei Geral da Copa*. The common polemics discussed in the newspaper involved special arrangements for FIFA during the 2013 Confederations Cup and 2014 World Cup, such as the special courts, tax breaks, changes in stadium names, the commercialisation of alcohol, concession prices for students, over-60s, and participants in programmes of income transfer (*Bolsa Família*), and the prizes for World Cup winners of the past. For instance, on the 17th of August 2011 the political commentator Luiz Carlos Azevedo informs about the initial steps in the formulation of the *Lei Geral da Copa* between the Minister of Sport, the Attorney General, and the Chief of Staff, and finish his comment by highlighting that 'one of the polemical topics [to be discussed in this meeting] is the sale of alcoholic drinks in stadiums' (Azevedo, 2011: 7). This frame becomes more salient on the 21st of September's sport section edition where the headline on the cover page read 'Stumbling Blocks' (*Pedras no Caminho*) and it emphasised alcohol sales alongside concession prices as the key polemics (Botão, 2011: 1). In the same edition on a double page aspect, the journalist Vagner Vargas lists all the polemics around the *Lei Geral da Copa* and alcohol legalisation appears as a key aspect as not only it was presented on third position in the list of polemics (out of six polemics) but it deserved a quote by a federal deputy who was against the legalisation claiming that it would be a risk to safety (Vargas, 2011: 8–9). On the 12th of October 2011 edition, the journalist Erich Decat informs about that the *Lei Geral da Copa* has been sent by the executive branch to the legislative (Chamber of Deputies) for analysis, and highlight that while the executive wants it to move faster and get it approved there are some polemical points in which alcohol sales features as one of them (Decat, 2011a). While the special committee at the Chamber of Deputies was analysing the *Lei Geral da Copa*, Vinicius Sassine writes that:

> today's meeting (between the Brazil's president, Ministry of Sport, and FIFA's representative Jerome Valcke) will serve for FIFA to intensify its pressure and force the government to cede (to their demands) (…) the principal point is concession prices (…) FIFA wants to end this benefit during the World Cup, as pressuring for the permission to sell alcoholic drinks in stadiums during game days.
> (Sassine, 2011: 6)

This quote introduces the second frame found on *Correio Braziliense* that portrayed the legalisations of alcohol as one of the key points in the arm-wrestle between FIFA and the Brazilian government. While FIFA had its own agenda, the Brazilian executive at the time under the Workers Party (*PT*) and the

Minister of Sport under the Communist Party (*PCdoB*) not only wanted to use the mega-event as part of their political agenda – specifically alongside its most important programme under *Bolsa Família* – but also keep some of the then current laws such as concession prices for students and over-60s valid even during the event. Reporting from Brussels (Belgium) as a special envoy following the then-President Dilma Roussef's state visit, Paulo Silva Pinto (2011) highlights that Dilma will face a hard game against FIFA in terms of complying with FIFA demands such alcohol sale and end of concession for students with balancing her desires to keep concession for over-60s. This arm-wrestle between the two parties got to a point in which it appeared that FIFA was the one in charge, specifically when the then Minister of Sport (Orlando Silva) became embroiled in corruption allegations, and Jerome Valcke gave an interview saying he was ready to meet with Dilma and the new representative, meaning a new Minister. This led the political correspondents covering from Brasília and Zurich to headline their coverage with '"Fired" by FIFA, maintained by Dilma' (Rothenburg et al., 2011: 2). This arm-wrestling got other parties involved as the legislative through the special committee decided to include other items into the *Lei Geral da Copa* such as a one-time prize money and a lifetime pension for the World Cup winners of 1958, 1962 and 1970 (Decat, 2011b), in a way that it framed this add-on by the legislative as a way to accommodate both FIFA demands such as the selling of alcohol, and the executive ones such as concession prices. The arm-wrestling got even more heated when Valcke gave an interview in March 2012 saying that the Brazilian government needed a 'kick up the ass' to accelerate the preparations for the Confederations Cup and World Cup, which led the sport editor of *Correio Braziliense* to headline the news as 'low blow to Brazil' and to add a quote by a Brazilian Senator (Álvaro Dias, then at the Social Democrat Party – *PSDB*) who said 'it is not from today that Brazil accepts humiliations. We need to defend Brazil from imposition attacks. They (FIFA) want to obtain vantages by affronting our legislations' (Botão, 2012a: 2–3). The arm-wrestle came to an *end* when the *Lei Geral da Copa* was approved by the Chamber of Deputies and promulgated by Dilma Roussef, nevertheless *Correio Braziliense* continued to frame it as having items in that law that were polemic such as the sale of alcohol in stadiums and making it salient by adding to the cover page of the 7th of March 2012 edition (Botão, 2012b: 1).

Inasmuch that violence stemming from the consumption of alcohol did not feature prominently as a frame on *Correio Braziliense* it is possible to assume that this causal effect was already ingrained in the readers' frame of reference because of past episodes in Brazilian football history. Therefore, *Correio Braziliense* did not need to re-emphasise it when framing the legalisation of alcohol during FIFA tournaments because audiences were already familiar with the rationale for its *banning* through the *Estatuto do Torcedor*. This was evident when reporting on the initial vote for the *Lei Geral da Copa* in the Chamber of Deputies, when Vargas (2012) highlighted that there was a 'big blunder' due to the absence of an article in the law that specifically legalised the commercialisation and consumption of alcohol in stadiums – a request by FIFA. This was stated in a feature box, clarifying that the law contained an item that suspended for the period of the Confederations Cup and World Cup the *Estatuto do Torcedor*'s article banning fans from carrying and using any object, drink, or illegal substance that could incite acts of violence. Nevertheless, between the Confederations Cup and the World Cup in 2013 *Correio Braziliense* ran a two-page feature headlined by 'Routine of Barbarism', in which the subheading reads: 'Brazil already has 13 deaths in clashes between organised fan groups in 2013, and it could break last year's *record*. Lack of punishment is cited by experts as the main cause of the situation' (Martimon, 2013: 8). While most of the two-page feature focus exclusively on Brazilian football, it highlights issues that could arrive in the World Cup because of some polemical points contained in the *Lei Geral da Copa* such as the waving of visa requirements for foreign fans, specifically Argentinians *Barra-Bravas* and English *Hooligans*. While alcohol was not singled out as cause for those violent episodes in this particular story, it has pointed that punishment for individuals causing violence is difficult to achieve as in some instances it is impossible to establish who actually committed the crime. Despite that, the clear identification of culprits through technology was used as a possible reason for changing the way *sentences* are given (from group to individual), which ultimately reinforces the frame that the *Estatuto do Torcedor* should be adapted to this new environment and therefore allowing for the consumption of alcohol in stadiums (Decat, 2011c). Notwithstanding, during the period of the World Cup there were some violent incidents around stadiums leading Jerome Valcke to blame the government and alcohol for the lack of security (Martimon and Cunha, 2014). Highlighting that alcohol consumption in stadium was a FIFA imposition, the journalists emphasised this contradiction by adding a quote from Valcke's interview where he states that 'I was impressed by the amount of alcohol people consumed. Many were intoxicated, and this can increase violence'. Finally, in one of the last news on the *Lei Geral da Copa*, Seffrin and Cunha (2014) reflect on legacies from the World Cup and highlight that alcohol commercialisation and consumption in stadiums is a divided legacy with some municipalities and states reverting to banning it, while others legalising it and having their publicly owned stadiums signing naming rights deals with a Brazilian brewery.

In sum, while the four stages described by Entman (1993) are not clearly evident in those news stories independently, it is possible to deduct them when looking at the collection of all stories associated with the historical links between alcohol and professional sport as discussed in the literature review, and in particular its more recent history in Brazil. For instance, the legalisation of alcohol was clearly defined as a problem in terms of the *Lei Geral da Copa* because it overruled a current legislation (*Estatuto do Torcedor*) that came about to solve serious problems of violence between organised fan groups. Moreover, the external imposition by FIFA rather than a true dialogue between all involved stakeholders (e.g., clubs, society, politicians, health and police experts, etc.) was framed as a cause for concern as it did not take into consideration the local (Brazilian) situation. While *Correio Braziliense* tried to frame the legalisation by looking at both positives and negatives in terms of moral judgement, there was a tendency to frame it negatively due to the historical aspect of violence and the external imposition by FIFA. Finally, it appears that the solution was present in the last article discussing the legacy of the World Cup when it was claimed that each state and municipality would be able to legislate and decide more locally to revert to banning alcohol or keep it legalised as it was during the tournament.

Conclusion

With more economical Global South countries hosting mega-events such as the Olympic and Paralympic Games, and FIFA Men's and Women's World Cups arguably there will be more instances in which *cultural shocks* will be encountered. While professional modern sport can be considered a by-product of European modernisation (Hobsbawm, 1983), and therefore some important aspects in terms of its cultural consumption such as its closer association with the alcohol industry is seen as *natural*, in other places this is understood as problematic. Insofar, sport media scholars have commonly analysed those *cultural shocks* by focusing on how international media frames those Global South localities, rarely the viewpoint of those shocks come from the local media. In a way, by analysing how a local newspaper in Brazil framed the legalisation of alcohol as a cultural shock, and therefore problematic for a Brazilian audience, sheds light on how those encounters between *global forces* such as FIFA and its partners as AB InBev and *local resistance* unfolded. As presented in the frame analysis, this particular newspaper explicitly framed alcohol legalisation as problematic because of being an external imposition by FIFA, and more subtly invoked audiences' cultural frame of reference regarding the association between alcohol and fan violence, to make a moral judgement about its negative aspect and ultimately reinforce this reality for its audience. Hence, what *Correio Braziliense* achieved through its different frames was to culturally control through its selection of news and salience to specific frames how its audience should comprehend and perceive the associations between alcohol, football, and violence. Consequently, their historical framing of alcohol as problematic in terms of violence in football fulfilled its *prophecy* when in one of the last news stories there was an admission by FIFA representatives to those links, ultimately giving credence to this discursively reality. In sum, this media reality (Luhmann, 2000) acted as the ultimate form of social control by educating and instilling cultural norms and behaviours to its audience.

Notes

1 In Italic as there is no formal prohibition according to the analysis by dos Reis (2012); the regulation falls into the state and municipal legal remit, rather than the federal sphere.

2 See the more recent legislation in the *Lei Geral do Esporte* (Presidência da República, 2023).

References

Al-Emadi, A, Sellami, A & Fadlalla, A (2022) The perceived impacts of staging the 2022 FIFA World Cup in Qatar. *Journal of Sport & Tourism* 26(1), 1–20.

Azevedo, L C (2011) Brasília-DF. *Correio Braziliense*, 17th August, p. 7.

Bandura, C, Giulianotti, R, Martin, J, et al. (2023) Alcohol consumption among UK football supporters: Investigating the contested field of the football carnivalesque. *Drugs: Education, Prevention and Policy*, OnlineFirst, 1–12.

Biblioteca Nacional Digital (2023) Brazilian digital library. Available from: https://memoria.bn.br/hdb/periodico.aspx (Accessed: 17 July 2023).

Botão, A (2011) Super Esportes. *Correio Braziliense*, 21st September, p. 1.

Botão, A (2012a) Golpe baixo no Brasil. *Correio Braziliense*, 3rd March, 2–3.

Botão, A (2012b) Depois do chute, Copa ganha lei. *Correio Braziliense*, 7th March, p. 1.

Cleland, J & Cashmore, E (2016) Football fans' views of violence in British football: Evidence of a sanitized and gentrified culture. *Journal of Sport & Social Issues* 40(2), 124–142.

Cody, K & Jackson, S (2016) The contested terrain of alcohol sponsorship of sport in New Zealand. *International Review for the Sociology of Sport* 51(4), 375–393.

Collins, T & Vamplew, W (2000) The pub, the drinks trade and the early years of modern football. *The Sports Historian* 20(1), 1–17.

Collins, T & Vamplew, W (2002) *Mud, Sweat and Beers: A Cultural History of Sport and Alcohol*. Oxford. Berg.

Correio Braziliense (2020) Correio Braziliense, 60 anos de história. Available from: https://www.correiobraziliense.com.br/app/noticia/cidades/2020/02/08/interna_cidadesdf,826717/correio-braziliense-60-anos-de-historia.shtml (Accessed: 29 August 2023).

Davies, F (2009) An investigation into the effects of sporting involvement and alcohol sponsorship on underage drinking. *International Journal of Sports Marketing and Sponsorship* 11(1), 20–40.

Decat, E (2011a) O marco zero da Copa no Congresso. *Correio Braziliense*, 12th October, p. 2.

Decat, E (2011b) Homenagem aos Heróis. *Correio Braziliense*, 26th November, p. 6.

Decat, E (2011c) O relator e o lobby do álcool. *Correio Braziliense*, 20th October, p. 6.

Dixon, K (2014) The football fan and the pub: An enduring relationship. *International Review for the Sociology of Sport* 49(3–4), 382–399.

Dixon, P & Garnham, N (2005) Drink and the professional footballer in 1890s England and Ireland. *Sport in History* 25(3), 375–389.

dos Reis, H (2012) Lei Geral da Copa, álcool e o processo de criação da legislação sobre violência. *Movimento* 18(1), 69–99.

Dun, S (2014) No beer, no way! Football fan identity enactment won't mix with Muslim beliefs in the Qatar 2022 World Cup. *Journal of Policy Research in Tourism, Leisure and Events* 6(2), 186–199.

Eick, V (2010) Neoliberal sports event? FIFA from the Estadio Nacional to the fan mile. *City* 14(3), 278–297.

Entman, R (1993) Framing: Toward clarification of a fractured paradigm. *Journal of Communication* 43(4), 51–58.

FIFA (2023) Welcome to the FIFA+ Archive. Available from: https://www.fifa.com/fifaplus/en/archive (Accessed: 29 August 2023).

Foucault, M (1969) *L'Archeologie du Savoir*. Paris. Gallimard.

Gaffney, C (2010) Mega-events and socio-spatial dynamics in Rio de Janeiro, 1919–2016. *Journal of Latin American Geography* 9(1), 7–29.

Gamson, W (1989) News as framing. *American Behavioral Scientist* 33(2), 157–161.

Gee, S (2014) Sport and alcohol consumption as a neoteric moral panic in New Zealand: Context, voices and control. *Journal of Policy Research in Tourism, Leisure and Events* 6(2), 153–171.

Gee, S, Batty, R & Millar, P (2021) Alcohol sponsorship and New Zealand regional rugby unions: Crisis point or business as usual? *International Journal of the Sociology of Leisure* 4, 155–175.

Gee, S & Jackson, S (2012) Leisure corporations, beer brand culture, and the crisis of masculinity: The Speight's 'Southern Man' advertising campaign. *Leisure Studies* 31(1), 83–102.

Gee, S, Sam, M & Jackson, S (2017) Content analyses of alcohol-related images during television broadcasts of major sports events in New Zealand. *International Journal of Sports Marketing and Sponsorship* 18(3), 230–245.

Goffman, E (1986) *Frame Analysis: An Essay on the Organization of Experience*. Hanover. University Press of New England.

Graber, D (1989) Content and meaning: What's it all about. *American Behavioral Scientist* 33(2), 144–152.

Graeff, B (2020) *Capitalism, Sport Mega Events and the Global South*. London. Routledge.

Graeff, B & Knijnik, J (2021) If things go South: The renewed policy of sport mega events allocation and its implications for future research. *International Review for the Sociology of Sport* 56(8), 1243–1260.

Graeff, B & Petersen-Wagner, R (2019) Pelé, Romário and Ronaldo: The social trajectories of celebrity politicians and the 2014 FIFA World Cup in Brazil. In: Bettine, M & Gutierrez, G (eds) *Esporte e Sociedade - Um olhar a partir da globalização*. São Paulo. Instituto de Estudos Avançados - USP, pp. 50–70.

Graeff, B, Gutierrez, D, Sardá, T, et al. (2019) Capable, splendorous and unequal: International media portrayals of Brazil during the 2014 World Cup. *Third World Quarterly* 40(4), 796–814.

Gutierrez, D & Bettine, M (2022) The international journalistic coverage of the Rio de Janeiro Olympic Games: Analysis by media framing. *Sport in Society* 25(1), 181–196.

Henderson, J (2014) Hosting the 2022 FIFA World Cup: Opportunities and challenges for Qatar. *Journal of Sport & Tourism* 19(3/4), 281–298.

Hobsbawm, E (1983) Mass-producing traditions: Europe, 1870–1914. In: Hobsbawm, E & Ranger, T (eds) *The Invention of Tradition*. Cambridge. Cambridge University Press, pp. 263–307.

IOC (2023) Olympic games. Available from: https://olympics.com/ioc/celebrate-olympic-games (Accessed: 29 August 2023).

IPC (2023) Paralympic events. Available from: https://www.paralympic.org/events (Accessed: 29 March 2023).

Ireland, R, Muc, M, Bunn C, et al. (2021) Marketing of unhealthy brands during the 2018 Fédération Internationale de Football Association (FIFA) World Cup UK broadcasts – a frequency analysis. *Journal of Strategic Marketing*, OnlineFirst, 1–16.

Jackson, S (2014) Globalization, corporate nationalism and masculinity in Canada: Sport, Molson beer advertising and consumer citizenship. *Sport in Society* 17(7), 901–916.

Kelly, S, Ireland, M, Mangan, J, et al. (2018) Can alcohol sponsorship be diluted by health messaging? *Sport in Society* 21(3), 434–451.

Lee Ludvigsen, J A (2022) *Football and Risk: Trends and Perspectives*. London. Routledge.

L'Equipe (2022) Le virage à 180° du Qatar et de la FIFA juste avant la Coupe du monde sur la vente d'alcool autour des stades. Available from: https://www.lequipe.fr/Football/Article/Le-virage-a-180-du-qatar-et-de-la-fifa-juste-avant-la-coupe-du-monde-sur-la-vente-d-alcool-autour-des-stades/1365593 (Accessed: 29 August 2023).

Lippmann, W (1922) *Public Opinion*. New York. Harcourt, Brace and Company.

Luhmann N (2000) *The Reality of the Mass Media*. Cambridge: Polity Press.

Martimon, A (2011) Rotina de Barbárie. *Correio Braziliense*, 1st September, pp. 8–9.

Martimon, A & Cunha, T (2014) Valcke culpa governo e álcool for falta de segurança. *Correio Braziliense*, 2nd July, p. 6.

Mason, T (1980) *Association Football and English Society: 1863–1915*. Sussex: The Harvester Press.

McCrae, N (2008) Football and beer in the 1960s: Transformation of the British brewing industry and its impact on local identity. *Sport in History* 28(2), 236–258.

Messner, M & Montez de Oca, J (2005) The male consumer as loser: Beer and liquor ads in mega sports media events. *Signs* 30(3), 1879–1909.

Müller, M & Gaffney, C (2018) Comparing the urban impacts of the FIFA World Cup and olympic games from 2010 to 2016. *Journal of Sport & Social Issues* 42(4), 247–269.

Nicholson, M, Hoye, R & Brown, K (2014) Alcohol and community football in Australia. *International Review for the Sociology of Sport* 49(3/4), 294–310.

Noel, J, Babor, T, Robaina, K, et al. (2016) Alcohol marketing in the Americas and Spain during the 2014 FIFA World Cup Tournament. *Addiction* 112, 64–73.

O'Brien, K & Kypri, K (2008) Alcohol industry sponsorship and hazardous drinking among sportspeople. *Addiction* 103, 1961–1966.

O'Brien, K, Ferris, J, Greenlees, I, et al. (2014) Alcohol industry sponsorship and hazardous drinking in UK university students who play sport. *Addiction* 109, 1647–1654.

Palmer, C (2014) Sport and alcohol – who's missing? New directions for a sociology of sport-related drinking. *International Review for the Sociology of Sport* 49(3–4), 263–277.

Palmer, C & Thompson, K (2007) The paradoxes of football spectatorship: On-field and online expressions of social capital among the 'grog squad'. *Sociology of Sport Journal* 24(2), 187–205.

Petersen-Wagner, R (2017a) Symbolic footprints: Media representations of host countries. In: Mataruna-dos-Santos, L J and Pena, B G (eds) *Mega Events Footprints: Past, Present and Future*. Rio de Janeiro. Engenho, pp. 319–344.

Petersen-Wagner, R (2017b) The football supporter in a cosmopolitan epoch. *Journal of Sport & Social Issues* 41(2), 133–150.

Petersen-Wagner, R (2017c) Cultural consumption through the epistemologies of the south: 'Humanization' in transnational football fan solidarities. *Current Sociology* 65(7), 953–970.

Petersen-Wagner, R, Filho, A R, Damiani, C, et al. (2018) CONMEBOL - Confederacion Sudamericana de Futbol. In: Chadwick, S, Parnell, D, Widdop, P, et al. (eds) *Routledge Handbook of Football Business and Management*. London. Routledge, pp. 459–472.

Petersen-Wagner, R & Ludvigsen, J A L (2023) Staging Olympic sustainability? A critical analysis of the IOC's framing of sustainable practices on YouTube. *Annals of Leisure Research*, OnlineFirst, 1–20.

Pinto, P S (2011) Jogo duro para Dilma. *Correio Braziliense*, 4th October, p. 1.

Presidência da República (2003) Lei N° 10.671, de 15 de Maio de 2003. Available from: https://www.planalto.gov.br/ccivil_03/leis/2003/l10.671.htm (Accessed: 31 August 2023).

Presidência da República (2012) Lei N° 12.663, de 5 de Junho de 2012. Available from: https://www.planalto.gov.br/ccivil_03/_ato2011-2014/2012/lei/l12663.htm (Accessed: 31 August 2023).

Presidência da República (2023) Lei N° 14.597, de 14 de Junho de 2023. Available from: https://www.planalto.gov.br/ccivil_03/_Ato2023-2026/2023/Lei/L14597.htm#art217 (Accessed: 31 August 2023).

Purves, R, Critchlow, N, Giulianotti, R, et al. (2022) Sport fan attitudes on alcohol: Insights from a survey of football supporters in Scotland and England. *Journal of Sport & Social Issues* 46(2), 199–218.

Rothenburg, D, Lyra, P, Silveira, I, et al. (2011) "Demitido" pela FIFA, mantido por Dilma. *Correio Braziliense*, 22nd October, p. 2.

Said, E W (1994) *Culture and Imperialism*. London. Vintage Books.

Said, E W (2003) *Orientalism*. London. Penguin Books.

Sassine, V (2011) FIFA discute ajustes na Lei da Copa. *Correio Braziliense*, 13th October, p. 6.

Scharfenort, N (2012) Urban development and social change in Qatar: The Qatar National Vision 2030 and the 2022 FIFA World Cup. *Journal of Arabian Studies* 2(2), 209–230.

Scheufele, D (1999) Framing as a theory of media effects. *Journal of Communication* 49(1), 103–122.

Seffrin, F & Cunha, T (2014) Herança Dividida. *Correio Braziliense*, 17th July, p. 3.

Statista (2021) Average paid circulation of selected newspapers in Brazil in December 2021. Available from: https://www.statista.com/statistics/261629/leading-newspapers-in-brazil-by-circulation/ (Accessed: 29 August 2023).

Tewksbury, D & Scheufele, D (2020) News framing theory and research. In: Oliver, M B, Raney, A & Bryant, J (eds) *Media Effects: Advances in Theory and Research*. 4th ed. London. Routledge, pp. 51–68.

The Guardian (2022) Qatar bans beer from World Cup stadiums after 11th-hour U-turn. Available from: https://www.theguardian.com/football/2022/nov/18/qatar-bans-beer-from-world-cup-stadiums-fifa-u-turn (Accessed: 29 August 2023).

The New York Times (2022) Ban on beer is latest flash point in World Cup culture clash. Available from: https://www.nytimes.com/2022/11/18/sports/soccer/world-cup-beer-qatar.html (Accessed: 29 August 2023).

Thompson, K, Palmer, C & Raven, M (2011) Drinkers, non-drinkers and deferrers: Reconsidering the beer/footy couplet amongst Australian Rules football fans. *The Australian Journal of Anthropology* 22(3), 388–408.

Vamplew, W (2016) Sport, industry and industrial sport in Britain before 1914: Review and revision. *Sport in Society* 19(3), 340–355.

Vargas, V (2011) Lei Geral da Copa provoca atritos. *Correio Braziliense*, 21st September, pp. 8–9.

Vargas, V (2012) Uma grande trapalhada. *Correio Braziliense*, 15th March, p. 5.

Vendrame, A (2016) When evidence is not enough: A case study on alcohol marketing legislation in Brazil. *Addiction* 112, 81–85.

Weaver, D (2007) Thoughts on agenda setting, framing, and priming. *Journal of Communication* 57(1), 142–147.

Wenner, L & Jackson, S (2009) Sport, beer, and gender in promotional culture: On the dynamics of a holy trinity. In: Wenner, L & Jackson, S (eds) *Sport, Beer, and Gender: Promotional Culture and Contemporary Social Life*. Zurich. Peter Lang, pp. 1–32.

6 Confronting Sectarianism in Contemporary Scottish Football
From Old Firm to New Challenges

Christie Scanlon

Introduction

Sectarianism can be defined as a complex of perceptions, attitudes, beliefs, actions, and structures, involving a negative mixing of religion with politics, sporting allegiance, and national identifications (Scottish Government, 2018). This negative aspect of sectarianism has been most associated with the Catholic-Protestant divide in Scotland and Northern Ireland, which has resulted in deep divides between communities, as well as a history of violence and discrimination. Sectarian divide in the West of Scotland date back to the mass emigration from Ireland during the emergence of the industrial revolution. This resulted in a large influx of Irish Catholics to Protestant-dominated Scotland, and over time has caused tensions and discrimination between the two communities (Vaughan, 2015). Political turbulence between the British and Irish governments has also exacerbated the symmetrical divisions between the two communities, with republicanism and unionism being used as political and social identity markers (May, 2015). Sectarianism has seemed to be entrenched in the social fabric of Scotland, with a variety of forms ranging from discrimination, prejudice, and violence. More recently, football and cultural parades have become proxies for sectarian conflict, with smaller factions using these as platforms to express their political leanings (Kelly and Bradley, 2021). This has caused a more modern resurgence of sectarianism to emerge, with symbols and songs being used to display one's allegiance.

It is important to note that sectarianism is a complex and multifaceted issue that has had a lasting impact on the West of Scotland. The long history of discrimination, prejudice, and violence during Irish migration serves as an important cue that sectarian behaviours are still deeply entrenched in the fabric of society (Hickman and Ryan, 2020). However, the need to criminalise such behaviour or to tackle the problem has been somewhat controversial, with many opposing opinions and perspectives on how to address the issue. Today, new communication tools such as social media and the internet have also become increasingly popular in allowing discrimination to be widely disseminated, with hate speech being used to incite violence (Cleland, 2014). As such, there is a need for greater awareness, education, and understanding of the issue to be established to help tackle sectarian behaviours. This chapter aims to provide an overview of the current understandings of sectarianism in Scotland, as well as looking at how the problem has been addressed over time. It will also outline key recommendations that should be considered to address this complex issue.

Unpacking Sectarianism

To fully understand sectarianism, we first must consider the roots of it by looking at its historical context. The origins of contemporary forms of sectarianism can be traced back to the sixteenth-century reformation and the subsequent conflict between various religious groups (Rosie, 2004). The division between Protestantism and Catholicism manifested itself throughout British society, with each side emphasising their own distinct identity. During the twentieth century, sectarianism was often used as a tool for political manipulation by those in power and this further entrenched the divisions in society (Rosie, 2004). Migration from Ireland into working class areas links to the spread of sectarian views, with political and religious tensions contributing to an environment of mistrust (Ghaill, 2001). Political loyalties and affiliations become associated with different religious denominations, creating an even deeper societal divide. Irish-Catholic-Republicans were often pitted against the Protestant-Unionists in a battle for control and power during a period where industrialisation of urban cities added further complexity to class relations (Vaughan, 2015).

The conflict in Northern Ireland during the 1970s and 1980s broadens the tensions between Catholics and Protestant communities during a period of civil unrest. Through this, religious identity became even more associated with political allegiance, with many Irish migrants in the UK connected to their Irish counterparts and their cultural background back in Ireland (Kelly, 2013). The 'Troubles' became a focal point on sectarian tensions in the West of Scotland, with people feeling an increased pressure to adhere to their religious beliefs and political leanings. To be clear, it is important to note that civil war in Northern Ireland was not symmetrical or war-torn in the same way in Scotland. It was instead a case of deep-rooted grievances and power struggles that was used to fuel social divisions (Hamilton-Smith and McArdle, 2013). This was compounded by football and other cultural events, which often saw Catholics or Protestants feeling the need to express their ideals and beliefs. Paraphernalia was also felt in other aspects of Scottish life, ranging from the workplace to education, to the role of the media in perpetuating divisions (Walls and Williams, 2005).

The sour intricacy of sectarian views in Scotland has led to many debates and discussions on how it is defined and understood. Interventions from academics, activists, and politicians have attempted to recognise and define the term; with discussions around the politics of identity, language, culture, and religion being commonplace (Bruce et al., 2005). Finn et al. (2008) indicate that Sectarianism has an 'omnifarious meaning' that does not fall easily into a single categorisation, leading to an increase in social stigmatisation and suspicion. This has been further intensified by the changing societal landscape in Scotland, with the introduction of devolution powers to Scottish Parliament, less Irish migration, and less religious commitment (Hamilton-Smith and McArdle, 2013). Consequently, academics such as Bruce et al. (2005) argue that sectarianism itself is an outdated form of religious conflict that does not impact the social and political dynamics of Scotland to date. Others, however, argue that the legacy of sectarian attitudes is deeply embedded within the culture of Scotland and is still a contemporary issue that needs to be addressed. This debate has led to more recent research and analysis from both sides of the argument, with a long history of current and previous studies (Bruce, 2019; McBride, 2018; Walls and Williams, 2005).

Mac an Ghail (2000) indicates that there is a 'whitewashing effect' of the Irish diaspora population and their past migration to the UK and America, meaning that an inter-ethnic animosity has become institutionalised in racial culture. This further perpetuates the negative connotations that are attached to the 'Sectarianism' with subtle and more overt forms of discrimination being more commonplace. What Mac an Ghail (2000) also implies is that certain cultural practices have been influenced by the conflict between Protestants and Catholics and defining 'Sectarianism' is more than just religious differences. Racism is noted as an important factor in understanding the complexity of sectarian views, with scholars like McBride (2018) suggesting that the 'anti-Irish racism' should be used to describe discrimination towards Irish culture. However, 'whiteness' seems to be a barrier to such discussion, as racism is often assumed to be linked with colour racism in contemporary academia. McBride (2022) also suggests that the forgotten aspects of the Irish diaspora have resulted in a partial blindness to discrimination experienced by those of Irish descent in Scotland. Such multifarious outlooks demonstrate the difficulty and multifaceted nature of understanding such phenomenon.

The deficit of academic work on sectarianism over the years has opened a narrow window for those wishing to challenge its existence. A various mix of opinions that fall under the 'sectarian' umbrella has resulted in a muddied view of what the term truly represents. Academics such as Whigham et al. (2021) argue that Sectarianism is based on race and religion that has been overtaken by more relevant factors such as politics and nationality. This suggests that Sectarianism has not disappeared, but rather adapted to the changing social and economic contexts. As such, Flint and Kelly (2013) suggest that two interpretations underline the existence of Sectarianism in Scotland: The first recognises the construction of identities within it, being that 'identity' is based on the expression of religious, national, and cultural beliefs. These identities belong to groups of people who define themselves through the prism of ethnoreligious and ethnic-nationalist origins embedded in the cultural fabric they exist. The second is the expression of Protestant/Loyalist/British/Catholic/Republican/Irish identities is thus socially and culturally driven and recognised in societal environments. Football stadiums and Orange Order (Protestant) and Republican (Catholic) Parades/Marches are examples of sect-specific rituals that permit the expression of these identities and continue to perpetuate a cycle of segregation and difference.

The need for theorising Sectarianism received Governmental Attention from the Advisory Group on Tackling Sectarianism in Scotland (AGTS) in 2012. A definition was designed to be inclusive and encourage a clear description of Sectarianism as a whole. This was meant to facilitate a better understanding of the current problem throughout Scotland and inform policy and public opinion on the issue. As mentioned, Sectarianism having multi-meanings is an inevitable consequence of its broad, contested, and dynamic nature. What this definition offers is a modern-day understanding of the term, as it moves away from archaic notions associated with religion and recognises that more complex issues are at play. Consequently, the AGTS defines Sectarianism in modern Scotland as:

> ... a complex of perceptions, attitudes, beliefs, actions, and structures, at personal and communal levels, which originate in religious difference and can involve a negative mixing of religion with politics, sporting allegiance, and national identifications.
> (Scottish Government, 2019)

Here, the definition is broad and inclusive enough to accommodate a variety of opinions and understandings. This is further compounded by the AGTS's attempt to move away from the traditional and cultural definitions associated with Sectarianism and focus on feelings, emotions, thoughts, and preferences. While religion remains an integral factor in understanding the concept, it is not the only influencing variable. It further expands to include facets such as politics and national identities, which have become increasingly relevant in the development of understanding Sectarianism throughout the West of Scotland. The ABTS definition offers a clear scope of how sectarian behaviours now exists, rather than one contested and capable of so many past interpretations. This point of reference will be used to explore the phenomenon and its current relevance below.

Sectarianism and Football Fandom

Football has been identified as a key cultural venue for sectarian behaviours, as it has been a focal point and site of competition between fans from both Celtic and Rangers FC (McBride, 2022). Such rivalry has been embedded in the cultural landscape of Glasgow, with fans from either side of the divide identifying strongly with their respective teams (Bradley, 2006). Old firm fixtures display a phenomenal level of enthusiasm, with flags and symbols being used to express identity and allegiance. Such cultural display marks a distinct point of difference between fans, and the ritualistic nature has been argued to be a significant factor in perpetuating sectarianism between the two teams (Bradley, 2017).

To be clear, Glasgow Celtic FC historically represents an Irish-Catholic background and Rangers FC has associated with a Scottish-Protestant identity. History and tradition have perpetuated rivalry, with stories of origin being used to further strengthen the distinction between the two clubs (Kelly and Bairner, 2018). Celtic was founded by Catholic priests in 1888 with the intention of providing a club for Irish immigrants, while Rangers have a longstanding reputation in the Scottish Protestant community. Over time, however, the distinction between Celtic and Rangers has been further defined by their respective fan bases and certain political and religious affiliations have become commonplace in how these teams are associated (Murray, 1984. We have seen, for example, the use of overwhelmingly Irish symbols and tricolour flags being used to represent Celtic FC, while Rangers have often been associated with Union Jacks and monarchy symbolism. Consequently, this has led to an identity divide between the two fan bases, with each faction displaying intense devotion and loyalty to their identity (Ormston et al., 2015).

While football is the emblematic nature of mainstream culture in Scotland, it is also a site behaviour and attitudes which can be seen to promote deviant behaviours (Nazir et al., 2022). The dynamics of the 'Old Firm' rivalry have been argued by many to further perpetuate existing tensions between the two clubs, with supporters becoming increasingly expressive in their display of identity. Bairner, (2015) notes that the cultural paraphernalia of the respective teams are used as a form of representation and provide a distinctiveness to which fans can adhere an ideological product of the historical Irish-British colonial conflict. What is interesting here is that football and fandom seem targeted as the ultimate platform of sectarianism, with the actions and behaviour of fans on and off the pitch being drawn into public discourse. Yet, the layers of complexity and power embedded in the cultural dynamics surrounding football have led to a more multifaceted understanding of the societal issues faced. As a result, sectarian antagonisms between Celtic and Rangers have become a norm in which fans often express their 'tribal' loyalties and politics. This has led to a situation in which sectarian views are deeply embedded into the cultural fabric of football fandom in the West of Scotland and are reinforced through fan rituals.

Sub-sections of supporters called 'Ultra' fans' co-ordinate atmosphere inside stadia through songs, displays, and chants which can often be seen as quite hostile (Doidge, 2017). This type of fandom is known to be highly polarised and robust in its expression of fan culture. Ultra-groups across Europe and around the world are well known for their tendency to go beyond what is traditionally accepted in a football setting. They are somewhat rebellious to the modification of fan culture to appease the views of those in authority. More recently, fans of both Celtic and Rangers and their formation of Ultra groups ('Green Brigade' & 'Union Bears) have been seen to further display the tribalism and divide between the two teams. Subsequently, authorities tend to challenge these groups as they often carry connotations of sectarian behaviour which can be seen as problematic (Brechbühl et al., 2017). This can be further understood in the use of symbols and Tifos that are often present at games and the lyrics of songs that are sung. Such fan culture is seen as an embodiment of the ongoing rivalry between these two teams and normalised in the environment of football, while others interpret it as a form of sectarian expression. This dichotomy has caused tension between authorities, supporters and clubs in Scotland with both sides unwilling to compromise on their beliefs (Deuchar and Holligan, 2010).

McBride (2018) mentions that a sense of moral panic is often created between Celtic and Rangers fans, and a sectarian dimension is often imprinted on both supporters. Songs and chants with sectarian connotations are used at football matches to display a sense of belonging and heritage that construct strong socio-political identity rooted in views that have been embedded over the years. The term '90 min bigot' has been coined to describe these attitudes and further highlights how sectarianism can infiltrate the footballing culture of Scotland (Kowalski, 2009). Yet, the contradiction of behaviours away from the game and how it is translated into everyday life remains contested and difficult to measure (Hamilton-Smith et al., 2015). While some may believe that this form of culture reflects a highly sectarian nature (Kelly, 2011) there are also other academics who feel that fan behaviour represents an exaggerated form of culture (Bradley, 2015). Consequently, football remains an increasingly contested cultural and social space where aspects of working-class culture are seen to be highlighted as problematical by authorities in contemporary Scotland (May, 2015).

Criminalisation of Sectarianism in Football

The need for criminalisation of sectarianism in football has been an increasing theme over the past decade and has been subject to much debate. Rangers and Celtic 'Shame Game' in 2011 along with sectarian threats to Neill Lennon was used as a puppet for the Scottish government to push for a policy that would criminalise sectarian behaviour in football (Flint and Kelly (2013). The Offensive Behaviour at Football and Threatening Communications (Scotland) Act 2012 (OBFA) was subsequently put into practice and sought to outlaw offensive behaviour and communication related to religious or racial hatred. The introduction of such law highlighted a desire from governing bodies in Scotland to challenge sectarianism head-on. While others felt that the legislation failed to consider the complexity of fan culture and its embedded dynamics. Fans of Celtic and Rangers were seen as an outlier in terms of regulation, as other public spaces were not subject to the same level of scrutiny, even though societal sectarianism arguably remains an issue (Lindores and Emejulu, 2019).

The UK's policies towards football-related offenses have seen varied levels of effectiveness, with notable successes in England, Wales, and Northern

Ireland (Hopkins and Hamilton-Smith, 2014). However, Scotland has arguably been slow to criminalise fans for sectarian issues due to a lack of consensus on whether there are problems that belong within the sporting sphere or wider society (Hamilton-Smith et al., 2011; Waiton, 2014). This somewhat has hindered Scotland's government to tackle sectarian behaviours which have arguably been normalised and embedded in football fan culture for years (Atkinson, 2022). Sectarian songs and chants in stadia have often been used to fuel division between the Celtic and Rangers, leading to a culture of polarisation that has been difficult for authorities to diffuse. Such social undertones of football culture are therefore deemed problematic by those in positions of authority, yet to many fans, it is a way for them to display their identity and football rituals. This is an ongoing dilemma for authorities in Scotland as they strive to create a culture of harmonious fandom (Hewer et al., 2017).

McBride (2017) and Bradley (2017) raise intriguing queries about the legal framework of OBFA. Central to this discussion is how 'cultural norms' can be used as a tool for hegemonic authority while simultaneously neglecting the deeper analysis of why such practices occur. Such paradoxes can be seen in the way Government has attempted to tackle sectarianism and framed as a football issue. Hamilton-Smith et al. (2015) research on this matter suggests that the only way to truly tackle sectarianism in Scotland is to foster an understanding of its social and cultural aspects as well as consider wider societal issues. Such challenge further highlight that football should not simply be seen as a source of blame when it comes to tackling sectarian behaviour, but rather viewed within a larger scope where its fans are seen as part of wider society. A lack of unified policy guidance has seen Scotland struggle to address issues, leading to confusion about how to police such behaviours. A lack of trust between the authorities, clubs, and fans has only further exacerbated the need for more effective policies and open dialogue that would bring about tangible results.

The subsequent repeal of the OBFA Act in 2018 has amplified the need for a refined way to tackle sectarian abuse at football. The Scottish government, however, is yet to put forward any policy that addresses this issue, leading to continuous speculation about the future of law and order in Scottish football at both grassroots and elite levels. Indeed, the 2015 Advisory Group on Tackling Sectarianism in Scotland report defines sectarianism in a much broader sense, looking beyond just religion to encompass other forms of bigotry (Law, 2015). Yet, any new policy must be carefully thought out to ensure a clear, nuanced understanding of the complexities of the issue. This would further promote tolerance and openness between different fanbases and create an environment where sectarianism can be challenged without fear of recrimination. Charities such as Kick it Out and Nil by Mouth are certainly examples of organisations that have been actively engaged in the fight against sectarianism and racism (Bruce, 2019). The need to continue such work is crucial if Scotland is to create a culture that not only values inclusivity but also actively challenges any form of discrimination.

As fandom is no longer confined to just football stadia, it is also important to consider how the rise of social media has impacted how we understand sectarianism and its propagation. Social media platforms have become increasingly used for both celebratory and abusive purposes, leading to a range of potential issues surrounding online behaviour (Boyle and Haynes, 2013). It is also important to remember that sectarianism can manifest in different ways, from explicit rhetoric on social media to implicit messages in the mainstream press (Kelly, 2011) Therefore, it is essential to consider how a broader media landscape can influence and reinforce sectarian abuse.

Social Media and Sectarian Abuse

It is increasingly evident that social media platforms and their popularity have become a hotbed for online abuse where identities can be hidden (Kavanagh et al., 2020). Several studies across a range of disciplines have explored online hate in ethnicity (Cleland, 2014), gender (Litchfield et al., 2018), and sexual orientation (Cleland et al., 2015). However, little attention has been on the issue of sectarian abuse. Central to 'Sectarianism' or 'anti-Irish Racism' in contemporary society is abuse directed towards Irish footballers who play professionally in Britain. Curren (2015) shows us that sectarian abuse of professional footballers is a problem that is not being taken seriously enough by social media platforms or the authorities. This lack of response from authorities is seen to further fuel abuse, especially among football fans who continue to be exposed to these attitudes through social media (Kilvington and Price, 2019).

While online sectarian abuse is not a new phenomenon, there is a tendency for it to be increasingly aggressive in nature with the anonymity that social media provides. This allows for a greater platform for fans to express their opinions while not being held accountable for them (Kearns et al., 2023). Social media, therefore, provides a space where criminogenic identities can be formed and sustained, as well as providing an audience for potential abusers to reinforce their views. Kilvington and Price (2018) highlight that the fear of reprisals, a lack of trust in social media platforms to act, and a feeling that nothing will be done even if it is reported all serve to further perpetuate the issue. Penfold and Cleland (2022) also add that there is a need for more awareness of the issue among both social media users and the public on racial discourse, meaning more trust and active participation is needed to tackle the issue. Consequently, the nature of sectarian behaviours being less visible in everyday life has led to a growth in abuse and hostility on social media platforms where there is no sense of accountability (Kilvington, 2021). This can lead to an increase in the perpetuation of 'sectarian' attitudes which could eventually filter into society.

Recently, instances of sectarian abuse on social media towards professional footballers in Britain have been widely documented and publicised. In 2021, it was reported that ex-Celtic defender Shane Duffy was the subject of sectarian abuse with death threats being made against him and his family (Sky Sports, 2021). In the same year, it was also reported that Irish footballer James McClean had been the target of sectarian abuse on social media, with death threats and racist abuse being directed towards him (Sky Sports, 2021). While McLean does not play for either Celtic or Rangers, his Irish heritage is seen to fuel sectarian abuse as many fans view him as a representative of the Irish identity that Celtic embodies. While abuse online is a disturbing trend, it serves yet another example of how sectarian abuse is perpetuated and how professional footballers are vulnerable to abuse. In turn, this has led to a lack of protection from social media companies and a decrease in trust in governing bodies and the criminal justice system to protect such victims (Cable et al., 2022).

It is anticipated that the effects of sectarianism on victims can be serious and long-lasting (Lindores & Emejulu, 2019). It is essential to have strategies in place to help those affected by online abuse. In 2022, a range of initiatives was created by football clubs across Britain to provide support for players who are being abused on social media (The FA, 2021). These include providing dedicated staff to monitor player accounts, creating and implementing regulations to punish those who send abusive messages, and providing mental health support services (The FA, 2021). Additionally, social media platforms have also been heavily criticised for their lack of action in tackling sectarian abuse. Irish players such as Aiden McGeady and James McClean have recently voiced their frustrations with the inaction of social media companies to protect their accounts from sectarian abuse (Sky Sports, 2020). Yet, despite this, social media companies have implemented various policies and tools to help control online abuse.

While this is a positive step in tackling sectarianism on social media, further research into the impact of these initiatives is needed to determine how effective they are. Fans are also urged to report any offensive material they come across to the relevant social media platform (Liston et al., 2023). This serves as a reminder that everyone has a responsibility to help tackle sectarianism and online abuse. However, the complexities of understanding sectarian behaviour and the difficulty of regulating online activity mean that it is a complex problem to tackle that requires a collaborative effort from all sectors of society. This includes social media companies, sport's governing bodies, the criminal justice system, and most importantly – football fans.

Conclusion

This chapter has considered the challenges of defining the historical contexts of Sectarianism and some of the conflicts and debates surrounding the topic in Scotland. While this is not an exhaustive account of a complex area of study and discussion, it has aimed to identify some of the critical issues and disagreements among scholars that should be considered when addressing research in this area. It has been apparent that Sectarianism in Scotland is multifaceted in how a collection of themes plays out. Yet, its understanding is rooted in the foundations of identity, religion, and culture. This chapter also strives to explore new ways in which Sectarianism is constructed. Some of the issues identified have provided an overview for further discussion and the different sociological and cultural understanding of the term (Finn, 1999). Moreover, the chapter has established how Sectarianism is perpetuated through social media. While this appears to be a difficult issue to address, it is important for all stakeholders to work together in order to help tackle sectarianism and online abuse. This will require a broader dialogue between those affected by sectarianism and those that can make a difference. Ultimately, this could lead to various changes in policy and regulations, as well as help to create a more inclusive and positive online environment.

The underpinning of Sectarianism in Scotland has only been made possible by the evolution of research that focuses on its reproduction within various cultural frameworks. What we do know is that the study of Sectarianism has shifted away from religious discrimination to cultural practices, with insufficient attention paid to the legacy of historic unequal power relations. Many more recent studies have focused on making sense of Sectarianism through conceptualising identities within football supporters of Glasgow Celtic and Rangers. This should be addressed to ensure that the discourse on Sectarianism is not confined to a single sport or city, while also separating it from its traditional associations with religion. Others argue that these criminalisation approaches have been somewhat controversial as they seem to target selected groups rather than a societal issue. It is important to note that it is not solely up to the criminal justice system to tackle sectarianism in Scotland. Other forms of engagement from a wide range of stakeholders including sports organisations, educational institutions, and social media companies are crucial for making effective change. This should include developing initiatives to support victims of online abuse by providing mental health services, as well as educating fans on how to report offensive material. Ultimately, this will help create a more cohesive society in Scotland that is more aware of what constitutes sectarian behaviour and how to prevent it. It is only through a collective effort that we can break the cycle of Sectarianism in Scotland.

References

Atkinson, C (2022) 'Football fans are not thugs': Communication and the future of fan engagement in the policing of Scottish football. *Policing and Society* 32(4), 472–488.

Bairner, A (2015) Bigotry, football and Scotland. *Soccer & Society* 14(4), 573–592.

Boyle, R & Haynes, R (2013). Sports journalism and social media: A new conversation? In: Hutchins, B & Rowe, D (eds) *Digital Media Sport*. New York. Routledge, pp. 204–218.

Bradley, J M (2006) Sport and the contestation of ethnic identity: Football and Irishness in Scotland. *Journal of Ethnic and Migration Studies* 32(7), 1189–1208.

Bradley, J M (2017) Sectarianism, anti-sectarianism and Scottish football. In: Reeves, K, Ponford, M and Gorman S (eds) *Managing Expectations and Policy Responses to Racism in Sport*, 1st Ed. London. Routledge, pp. 82–97.

Brechbühl, A, Schumacher Dimech, A, Schmid, O N & Seiler, R (2017) Escalation vs. non-escalation of fan violence in football? Narratives from ultra fans, police officers and security employees. *Sport in Society* 20(7), 861–879.

Bruce, S (2019) *Sectarianism in Scotland*. Edinburgh. Edinburgh University Press.

Bruce, S, Glendinning, T, Paterson, I & Rosie, M (2005). Religious discrimination in Scotland: Fact or myth? *Ethnic and Racial Studies* 28(1), 151–168.

Cable, J, Kilvington, D & Mottershead, G (2022). 'Racist behaviour is interfering with the game': Exploring football fans' online responses to accusations of racism in football. *Soccer & Society* 23(8), 880–893.

Cleland, J (2014) Racism, football fans, and online message boards: How social media has added a new dimension to racist discourse in English football. *Journal of Sport and Social Issues* 38(5), 415–431.

Cleland, J (2015) Discussing homosexuality on association football fan message boards: A changing cultural context. *International Review for the Sociology of Sport*, 50(2), 125–140.

Curran, C (2015) The migration of Irish-born footballers to England, 1945–2010. *Soccer & Society* 16(2–3), 360–376.

Deuchar, R & Holligan, C (2010) Gangs, sectarianism and social capital: a qualitative study of young people in Scotland. *Sociology* 44(1), 13–30.

Doidge, M (2017) 'The birthplace of Italian communism': Political identity and action amongst Livorno fans. In: *Fan Culture in European Football and the Influence of Left Wing Ideology*. London. Routledge, pp. 142–157.

Finn, GP (1999) Sectarianism and Scottish education. In: Bryce, TGK and Humes, WM (eds) *Scottish Education*. Edinburgh: Edinburgh University Press, pp. 897–907.

Finn, G, Uygun, F, & Johnson, A (2008, August). Sectarianism and the Workplace. In *Report to The Scottish Trade Union Congress and the Scottish Government*. Available from: http://www. stuc.org.uk/files/Reports/Sectarianism/STUC08. pdf.

Flint, J & Kelly, J (2013). Football and bigotry in Scotland. In Flint, J & Kelly, J (eds) *Bigotry, Football and Scotland*. Edinburg. Edinburgh University Press, pp. 3–18.

Ghaill, M M (2000). The Irish in Britain: The invisibility of ethnicity and anti-Irish racism. *Journal of Ethnic and Migration studies* 26(1), 137–147.

Ghaill, MMA (2001). British critical theorists: The production of the conceptual invisibility of the Irish Diaspora. *Social Identities* 7(2), 179–201.

Hamilton-Smith, N, Bradford, B, Hopkins, M, Kurland, J, Lightowler, C, McArdle, D & Tilley, N (2011). An evaluation of football banning orders in Scotland. Scottish Government Social research report. Available at: http://www.scotland.gov.uk/Resource/Doc/354566/0119713.pdf.

Hamilton-Smith, N & Hopkins, M (2013). The transfer of English legislation to the Scottish context: Lessons from the implementation of the Football Banning Order in Scotland. *Criminology & Criminal Justice* 13(3), 279–297.

Hamilton-Smith, N. & McArdle, D (2013). *England's Act, Scotland's shame, and the limits of law*. Edinburgh. Edinburgh University Press, pp. 130–144.

Hewer, P, Gannon, M & Cordina, R (2017). Discordant fandom and global football brands: 'Let the people sing'. *Journal of Consumer Culture* 17(3), 600–619.

Hickman, M J & Ryan, L (2020) The "Irish question": marginalizations at the nexus of sociology of migration and ethnic and racial studies in Britain. *Ethnic and Racial Studies* 43(16), 96–114.

Hopkins, M & Hamilton-Smith, N (2014) Football banning orders: The highly effective cornerstone of a preventative strategy? In *Football Hooliganism, Fan Behaviour and Crime: Contemporary Issues*. London. Palgrave Macmillan UK, pp. 222–247.

Kavanagh, E., Jones, I & Sheppard-Marks, L (2020) Towards typologies of virtual maltreatment: Sport, digital cultures & dark leisure. In: Silk, M, Millington, B, Rich, E & Bush, A (eds) *Re-Thinking Leisure in a Digital Age*. London. Routledge, pp. 75–88.

Kearns, C, Sinclair, G, Black, J, Doidge, M, Fletcher, T, Kilvington, D, Liston, K, Lynn, T & Rosati, P (2023) A scoping review of research on online hate and sport. *Communication & Sport* 11(2), 402–430.

Kelly, J (2011) 'Sectarianism' and Scottish football: Critical reflections on dominant discourse and press commentary. *International Review for the Sociology of Sport* 46(4), 418–435.

Kelly, J (2013) Popular culture, sport and the 'hero'-fication of British militarism. *Sociology* 47(4), 722–738.

Kelly, J & Bairner, A (2018). The 'talk o' the toon'? An examination of the Heart of Midlothian and Hibernian football rivalry in Edinburgh, Scotland. *Soccer & Society* 19(5–6), 657–672.

Kelly, J & Bradley, J M (2021) Celtic FC's 1967 Lisbon Lions: Why the European Cup victory of the first club from Britain was a defining moment for the Irish diaspora in Scotland. In: Bandyopadhyay, K & Naha, S (eds) *Moments, Metaphors, Memories*. London. Routledge, pp. 145–159.

Kilvington, D & Price, J (2018) From backstage to frontstage: Exploring football and the growing problem of online abuse. In: Lawrence, C & Crawford, G (eds) *Digital Football Cultures*. London. Routledge, pp. 69–85.

Kilvington, D & Price, J (2019) Tackling social media abuse? Critically assessing English football's response to online racism. *Communication & Sport* 7(1), 64–79.

Kilvington, D (2021) The virtual stages of hate: Using Goffman's work to conceptualise the motivations for online hate. *Media, Culture & Society* 43(2), 256–272.

Kowalski, RI (2009). Anti-Englishness and Sectarianism in Scottish Sport and Society: the'90 Minute Bigots'. In Hammarlund, KG (ed) *Borders as Experience*. Halmstad. Forskning i Halmstad, pp. 136–162.

Law, A (2015). Sectarianism, criminalisation and the civilising process in Scotland. In: Croall, H, Mooney, G & Munro, M (eds) *Crime, Justice and Society in Scotland*. London. Routledge, pp. 99–114.

Lindores, S & Emejulu, A (2019) Women as sectarian agents: Looking beyond the football cliché in Scotland. *European Journal of Women's Studies* 26(1), 39–53.

Liston, K, Kilvington, D, Black, J, Doidge, M, Fletcher, T, Kearns, C, Lynn, T & Sinclair, G (2023) A critical analysis of past and present campaigns to challenge online racism in English professional football. In: Awan, I & Zempi, I (eds) *Hate Crime in Football: How Racism Is Destroying the Beautiful Game*. Bristol University Press, pp. 83–102.

Litchfield, C, Kavanagh, E, Osborne, J & Jones, I (2018) Social media and the politics of gender, race and identity: The case of Serena Williams. *European Journal for Sport and Society* 15(2), 154–170.

May, A (2015) An 'anti-sectarian'act? Examining the importance of national identity to the 'offensive behaviour at football and threatening communications (Scotland) act'. *Sociological Research Online* 20(2), 173–184.

McBride, M (2018) The contemporary position of Irish Catholics in Scotland. In: Davidson, N, Liinpää, M, McBridge, M & Virdee, S (eds) *No Problem Here: Understanding Racism in Scotland*. Edinburgh. Luath Press, pp. 69–89.

McBride, M (2022). Nationalism and "sectarianism" in contemporary Scotland. *Ethnic and Racial Studies* 45(16), 335–358.

Murray, B (1984) *The Old Firm: Sectarianism, Sport and Society in Scotland*. Edinburgh: John Donald Publishers Ltd.

Nazir, T, James, K, Abdurahman, M & Al-Khazraji, H S (2022) Pakistani support for Glasgow's Old Firm football clubs. *Soccer & Society* 23(7), 784–804.

Ormston, R, Curtice, J, Hinchliffe, S & Marcinkiewicz, A (2015) A subtle but intractable problem? Public attitudes to sectarianism in 2014. *Scottish Affairs* 24(3), 266–287.

Penfold, C, & Cleland, J (2022) Kicking it out? Football fans' views of anti-racism initiatives in English football. *Journal of Sport and Social Issues* 46(2), 176–198.

Rosie, M (2004) *The Sectarian Myth in Scotland: Of Bitter Memory and Bigotry*. Basingstoke. Springer.

Sky Sports (2020). James McClean on sectarian abuse: People need to be held responsible. *Sky Sports*. Available from: https://www.skysports.com/football/news/11701/12028079/james-mcclean-on-sectarian-abuse-people-need-to-be-held-responsible (Accessed: 22 August 2023).

Sky Sports (2021) Shane Duffy: Celtic Defender shares sectarian online abuse received on Instagram, Sky Sports. Available at: https://www.skysports.com/football/news/11787/12225719/shane-duffy-celtic-defender-shares-sectarian-online-abuse-received-on-instagram (Accessed: 08 January 2024).

The FA (2021) The FA's new equality, diversity and inclusion strategy 2021–2024. *The FA*. Available from: https://www.thefa.com/news/2021/oct/08/a-game-for-all-fa-equality-diversity-inclusion-strategy-2021-2024-20210810 (Accessed: 22 August 2023).

The Scottish Government (2018) Legal definition of Sectarianism Working Group: Final report. *Scottish Government*. Available from: https://www.gov.scot/publications/final-report-working-group-defining-sectarianism-scots-law/ (Accessed: 22 August 2023).

The Scottish Government (2019) Scottish Social Attitudes Survey 2014: Public attitudes to sectarianism in Scotland. *Scottish Government*. Available from: https://www.gov.scot/publications/scottish-social-attitudes-survey-2014-public-attitudes-sectarianism-scotland/pages/4 / (Accessed: 22 August 2023).

Vaughan, G (2015) The Irish Famine in a Scottish perspective 1845–1851. *Mémoire (s), identité (s), marginalité (s) dans le monde occidental contemporain. Cahiers du MIMMOC*, (12). Available from: https://journals.openedition.org/mimmoc/1763.

Waiton, S (2014) Football fans in an age of intolerance. In Hopkins, M & Treadwell, J (eds) *Football Hooliganism, Fan Behaviour and Crime: Contemporary Issues*. London. Palgrave Macmillan UK, pp. 201–221.

Walls, P & Williams, R (2005) Religious discrimination in Scotland: A rebuttal of Bruce et al.'s claim that sectarianism is a myth. *Ethnic and Racial Studies* 28(4), 759–767.

Whigham, S, Kelly, J & Bairner, A (2021) Politics and football fandom in post-'indyref' Scotland: Nationalism, unionism and stereotypes of the 'Old Firm'. *British Politics* 16, 414–435.

7 Cultural Extraction and Subcultural Resistance in US Professional Soccer
If You're Not Anti, You're Pro

Chris W. Henderson and Pratik Nyaupane

Introduction

Before the 2019 season the organizers of the top flight of men's professional soccer in the US – Major League Soccer (MLS) – instituted a ban on "political" signage at their games. A primary target of the ban was the Iron Front mark, a circle with three arrows pointing to the left (Figure 7.1). After originating in 1930s Germany among outlawed groups that confronted National Socialism, the Iron Front has been deployed in many national contexts to represent anti-fascism. It has been a regular part of fan displays in Portland, Oregon since Portland Timbers FC reformed in the mid-1990s. Its most prominent use is a large banner flown in the Timbers Army organized fan group that features the iconic local statue Portlandia and with its trident's prongs replaced by the three arrows (Figure 7.2). The team management of Portland Timbers FC (PTFC) extended MLS's ban to the games of its National Women's Soccer League (NWSL) team Portland Thorns FC, even though the women's league did not restrict the symbol.

The ban and attempts at enforcement set off a season of resistant practices among the Rose City Riveters, the independent organized fan group for the Thorns, and their counterparts in the Timbers Army. When challenged by fans, MLS and PTFC framed the policy as necessary,

> to support the overwhelming majority of MLS fans who come to our stadiums to enjoy a soccer game. All of our fans and supporters are important to us and we will continue to engage with them to ensure we deliver an incredible experience for all.

They clarified that the Iron Front mark was outlawed because of its associations with "ANTIFA" and that other symbols used by the fan groups, in particular the rainbow pride flag, were not "political" and thus permitted (Thompson, 2019). The protests against the ban forced MLS to abandon its policy following the 2019 season.

Three years later in 2022, MLS enacted policies aimed at curtailing fan use of flares and other forms of fandom, including the "puto" chant at Banc

DOI: 10.4324/9781003453062-7

Figure 7.1 Iron Front Patch, Portland, May 2019. Image courtesy of Chris W. Henderson.

of California stadium in Los Angeles. A chant originating from Mexican club football, supporters start drumming up noise as the opposing goalkeeper sets to take a goalkick. As they approach and kick the ball, fans crescendo into a roaring "putoooo" in unison. The word is a vulgar term in Spanish and has many different interpretations often used in a pejorative manner. In the case of the football chant, it is perceived as a homophobic slur, translating to male prostitute. It has been prevalent in Mexican football, but in the last decade came under global scrutiny as it became a broader issue during Mexican national team matches, even those at the 2018 FIFA Men's World Cup in Russia. FIFA and the Mexican federation have been criticized for their inaction to deal with the chant, but in 2021 FIFA fined the Federation $65,000 and two match ban on supporters. The Federation then enacted a policy of handing out five year bans to fans caught engaging with the derogatory chant.

On April 29, 2018, Los Angeles FC (LAFC) hosted Seattle Sounders FC for Los Angeles' first ever home match at Banc of California Stadium. As the city's older team, LA Galaxy, which is located in suburban Carson, and catered to a suburban White audience throughout the area, LAFC meticulously crafted a team that would market itself as the inner city and Brown team. The opener was an historical moment for soccer fans from a variety of cultural backgrounds in LA, but for many, the experience was clouded by the infamous "Puto" chants. The 3252, the union of LAFC's supporter groups which includes significant numbers of Latino/a/x fans denied that it was their members engaging in the chant and emphasized that homophobia has no place at LAFC or in football (Velez, 2018). FIFA and CONCACAF, the governing body of football in North and Central America have denounced and discouraged the chant, while it continues on occasion (Balta, 2018).

Cultural Extraction and Subcultural Resistance in US Soccer 79

Figure 7.2 Portlandia Iron Front Banner, Portland, May 2019. Image courtesy of Chris W. Henderson.

As American soccer aimed to brand itself in a liberal progressive lens, the puto chant became the ultimate infraction. It was clamped down on by teams, the league, and the media. As Black and Brown players regularly face racism from opposing players and fans, groups of liberal White fans continue to preface homophobia as the premiere issue in the stands, targeting Latino/a/x, and specifically fans from Mexico or of Mexican descent. This presumption is problematic for two reasons. First, homophobia and the puto chant isn't indicative of Mexican culture, it is an aspect of Mexican stadium culture that is perpetuated by some. Second, it ignores that homophobia exists in White American sport settings, where it remains a rampant issue as Men's professional sports in the US has been a hostile space for both gay athletes and fans. Supporter groups such as the 3252 of LAFC, continue to counter these narratives as they express themselves as anti-homophobia while showing up in the stands as unapologetically diverse and Latino/a/x.

For the White American fanbase of soccer, the chant is associated with identity, one that is tainted in racism and xenophobia. They frame Latino/as fans as portrayed too aggressive and homophobic, while believing that Americans consume the sport in a more civilized manner. After many failed attempts to reach beyond White audiences, MLS is thrilled that LAFC attracts Latino/a/x fans and leverages their presence and culture, but also pacifies and "whitens" those cultural performances, while strictly policing Latino/a/x fans.

The contestations over fan culture in Portland and Los Angeles are indicative of a process that we call "cultural extraction." Cultural extraction occurs when dominant commercial institutions claim subcultural practices as their own products, while simultaneously policing integral elements of the same subculture because they challenge the institutions' efforts to create a "depoliticized" environment. In American soccer, cultural extraction takes the form of incorporating subculture generated by marginalized communities into inclusionary branding by reducing practices with distinct resistant politics to identity-based spectacle in support of consumer-based team support. Since the MLS's formation in the 1990s, US soccer leagues have primarily targeted an aspirational White suburban audience, selling themselves not as a reflection of local community, but rather as a signifier of social class attainment. Far from embracing the subcultural roots of American soccer, MLS and NWSL established their brands through neutral corporate signifiers unmarked by ethnic and racial difference, which were always already coded as White, cisgender, and professional class. As the leagues generally failed to attain enough financial capital to satisfy the needs of their corporate founders, they have made efforts to incorporate fan subcultures that originate outside of the US professional class.

Among their targets were independent supporter groups in Los Angeles and Portland that create expressive culture rooted in transnational traditions that include stadium performances of songs, dances, and displays. In both cases, fans enact communities that sustain the lives of marginalized people within the group and provide a platform for resistant politics. In Portland this includes radically feminist and queer fandom, in Los Angeles, a diversity of Latino/a/x communities. Team owners extract selected elements from fan subculture to include in their branding, claiming ownership over fan subculture because it is connected to the teams they control.

The purpose of cultural extraction is to at once weaken the resistant power of subcultural practices and symbols and capitalize on them by incorporating some subcultural elements and strictly policing others. Under the guise of a universalized inclusion, soccer companies frame fan subcultures as depoliticized identity-based spectacle, representative of a committed, inclusive, and respectable fandom. In Portland this entailed endorsing the Riveters and Timbers Army's rainbow iconography as distinct from anti-fascism, in Los Angeles this included the use of symbols from a variety of Latin American cultures while Latino/a/x fans faced the brunt of increased securitization of Banc of California Stadium. The soccer brands use fan images, symbols, and performances without consent or consultation for how they are portrayed in marketing campaigns.

Without fully engaging with the resistant politics that grounds fan subcultures and instead divorcing them from the community from which it comes, soccer companies fail to create more inclusive and tolerant environments. When the soccer brands attempt to extract culture that does not belong to them for the purpose of advertising depoliticized spectacle, they find themselves challenged by the very people they seek to include. The organized fan groups find ways to maintain their culture for resistant purposes and use conflicts with the owners to strengthen subcultural community and political organizing. Conflicts like these are part of what Hall (1981: 233) calls "a continuous and necessarily uneven and unequal struggle, by the dominant culture to constantly disorganize and reorganize popular cultures." In what follows, we trace the process of cultural extraction in Los Angeles and Portland to illuminate its dangers and potential resistances to it.

Methods

To understand the extractive culture, we combine autoethnograpic experiences among organized fan groups with close readings of club marketing materials, public statements, and press reports. As members of the organized supporters groups, we adopted, "co-performative witnessing" an evidence-gathering technique defined by Conquergood (2013) and later refined by Peña (2011) and Madison (2011, 2013). Co-performative witnessing emphasizes "listening to and being touched by" (Conquergood, 2013: 37) experiences in the field. Instead of observing at a distance, we performed alongside fans in stadiums paying close attention to affective, tactile, and embodied impacts of participation in fandom. In Portland, this work was supplemented by 30 interviews with Rose City Riveters and Timbers Army members that enabled interlocutors to offer expertise on their fandom experiences.

In our analysis, we adopt Dolan's (2012) notion of "critical generosity" that centers the historical context and available resources available in the production of culture. We avoided measuring whether fan performances met cultural norms of authenticity and instead considered what they might mean for their creators and their audience materially and culturally. This meant taking into account the labor the performances entailed and who they impact. For fan cultures – in which ideas of authenticity play a significant role in traditional evaluation practices – critical generosity allowed us to carefully consider fan actions inside and outside the stadium without determining whether or not fans were celebrating and supporting in ways deemed proper by other fans, team owners or normative codes.

We Don't Need a Sign: Anti-Indentarian Fan Subculture

The Portland and Los Angeles fan groups locate themselves in the transnational tradition of grassroots fan organizations common in South America and Europe. On gameday, they commandeer the atmosphere of the stadium with their presence and performance through chants and visual displays (tifo). Many fan organizations, particularly in Italy, Germany, and Iberia, took on explicitly far right and far left political affiliations in the 1970s and 1980s (Lee, 2022; Kuhn, 2011). The fan groups in Portland draw parallels through their performances and symbols to the socialist, anti-fascist, and leftist fan organizations elsewhere, especially FC St. Pauli in Germany. The groups in Los Angeles mix European anti-fascist traditions with a heavy influence of Latin American barra culture. Fans grounded in various diasporas express their subcultures and the material representation of where they come from. On any given day flags from Colombia, Palestine, Ecuador, Guatemala, Germany among others fill what is now called BMO Stadium.

US fan-generated culture is often subcultural in a way that Hebdige (1979: 18) argues, "interrupt(s) the process of normalization (with) gestures, movements toward speech which offends the 'silent majority,' which challenges the principle of unity and cohesion." Fan groups align with anti-establishment politics through disruptive performances and aesthetics that defy mainstream culture and resist commercialization. While crafting cultural objects and spectacles to support the team, they intentionally maintain independence from the team's commercial framework.

Organized fan groups seek to crystallize, objectify, and communicate group experience as distinct from the dominant gendered professional class culture of the corporate structures of MLS and NWSL. At Thorns matches, these efforts are led by queer women, while in Los Angeles, fan groups seek to reflect and empower the complex diasporic multiculturalism of their city. The fans' collective performances are not incidental or accidental but, instead grounded in "cultural labor," the "constant and strenuous work" done by marginalized groups to create culture and community (Bailey, 2013; Kelley, 1997). This labor includes the physical work done during performances, the creative aesthetic practices that instill the performances with resistant politics, and the all-volunteer coordination work done in between gamedays that brings performances into being. They maintain their culture through what Taylor (2003) calls embodied "acts of transfer" that move it from place to place and body to body across time and space through repeated expressive practice. They preserve memory and history while building a community of mutual support, producing reservoirs of feelings, embodied traditions, and an enduring community that does not rely upon the companies that run the teams for its validation or continuance. They understand their affective, corporeal, and communal productivity beyond any financial capital they might generate.

Therefore, resistant politics are not ancillary, but essential to how the grassroots fan organizations function. They expend economic and social capital to sustain their subcultural practices independent of the team's corporate entities. This involves acts of welcome and boundary patrol on gameday and elsewhere that enable the group's performance traditions and inclusionary culture to be passed on. The material and performative culture generated by the group holds value in part because of its establishment outside of the team's corporate hierarchy. Fan groups resist maneuvers by the teams and leagues to extract their culture. These conflicts require additional labor, but also strengthen resistant stances, build community among supporters, and enhance preparation for further political action.

Portland: Anti-fascist Queerness

The Riveters formed in 2013 long before the Thorns played a game or even had a name. Founded in part by women members of the Timbers Army who could not attain leadership positions because of gendered forms of power, the Riveters made radical feminism and queerness an integral part of their organization. As with other fan subcultures, the Riveters' performance's organic collective structure, unapologetically confrontational vocalization, and intent to commandeer the stadium's atmosphere builds community in place and challenges many of the professional class conventions of the stadium. Additionally, unlike the male-dominated groups of men's soccer, the Riveters' organized presence, gender-troubling appearances, intentional inclusionary behavior, and demonstrative queer love also interrupts the coherence of the performance of sports fandom with male sex, toxic masculinity, and heterosexual desire. The Riveters' performance is unapologetically queer, led and organized substantially by queer people, performed by a group that includes a significant majority of women in a space that is normatively hostile to anything other than cis-masculinity and heteronormative conventions (Henderson, 2015). The radical queerness of the Riveters' space is not limited to individual representation of homosexual identity and its visible symbols like the rainbow flag. Rather, the North End's queerness is grounded in, "what community members do, as opposed to who they are" (Bailey, 2013: 23). They express gender and sexuality, including homosexual desire, in ways that reject dominant ideologies, while creating a community that calls alternate ways of being into existence, disrupts normative codes of belonging, and challenges marginalization in place. While people who identify as LGBT make up a significant part of the group and form the basis for its inclusionary practices, much of what makes the Riveters radically queer is the insistence on what one Riveter called, "celebrating the differences as long as you're into equality and justice."

The group's performance runs counter to the dominant postfeminist heteronormative image of US women's sport challenging notions of how they as women and queer people are supposed to act in public (McDonald, 2008; Allison, 2018). Among the Riveters, femininity is not docile, achievement-based and family-friendly, it is aggressive, confrontational, and grounded in anti-establishment politics. The Riveters take space where dominant modes of gender performance prescribe them unwelcome by engaging what Muñoz (1999) theorizes as disidentification. They "negotiate a phobic majoritarian sphere" by adopting and changing the meaning of fan practices, as "powerful sites of self-creation" (p. 4). Or as one Riveter put it, "Just being rowdy. The sort of idea that women are hysterical if they're rowdy. We're very disruptive. The rest of the league … most people don't like the Riveters." Or as another stated, "It represents the way women are supposed to act. We're loud and we're taking up space and this is what we do. We're supporting our team. We're putting all of our energy into this." By commandeering the normative space of the stadium, they publicly refuse gender-based marginalization. In the process, they undermine neoliberal ideas of progress for oppressed people being marked by acquiescence to dominant forms of culture.

The Riveters' performances draw criticism, especially when they travel to away matches en masse, a practice common in men's soccer, but generally absent from women's soccer. In line with professional class heteronormativity, a common complaint is that the Riveters' presence, particularly their language, has an adverse effect on children. There is a sense among the Riveters that the mere presence of uninhibited women unnerves teams and fans. One explained it this way,

> A lot of the fights … at the beginning of the league were in reaction to the Rose City Riveters being the way that we are. Being comfortable flipping off players, being comfortable using swear words in chants, being comfortable heckling. Not sitting there politely with our hands crossed watching a match like it was a tennis match.

The Riveters ridicule moves to police their behavior. They produced a kids' scarf that reads "Think of the Children" on one side and "I Survived the F Bombs" on the other. Another scarf, in support of an animal shelter, proclaimed "Two Balls Is Too Many" using vulgarity to draw specific attention to the genders of the players and many of the fans. By intentionally mocking concerns about language, children, respectability, and femininity, the Riveters show that they recognize the ways that they unsettle notions of how women can behave in public and make it a foundation to their culture.

The Riveters' unapologetically anti-identitarian queerness includes how they deploy political symbols like the rainbow flag. Their displays ferociously

Figure 7.3 Sunday White with Gloria, June 21, 2019. Photo by Darren Lloyd/ 107IST.

take up space rather than pleading for tolerance. As one Riveter stated, "That Love is Love, that's super nice, that's nice that you do that but that's not (us). We're here, we're queer. You know, this is what we do." In 2019, their annual Pride scarf included the image of a stonewall on one side with rainbow bricks as well as brown and black one and the words Pride is a Riot on the other. The scarf references the modern gay rights movement's genesis in the direct action of the Stonewall Riot rather than more assimilative measures that followed. The accompanying Pride tifo read Loud, Proud, and Unbowed. Importantly the rainbow flag does not fly in the Riveters' North End only during Pride Month in June. The symbol, along with other flags representing other non-normative sexualities and genders, is everywhere at each match, including on the *capo* stand in the form of a massive rainbow flag that the group calls "Gloria" (Figure 7.3).

When the ban on the Iron Front came down, the Riveters refused any implication that the politics of anti-fascism could be separated from those of queerness embodied in their use of the rainbow flag. Although the Riveters use of the Iron Front chronologically follows its deployment by the Timbers Army, the symbol carries added weight for them. The Timbers Army is grounded in anti-fascist resistance but also hyper-masculinity with a history of whiteness and misogyny. It is possible therefore for MLS to more easily disconnect the anti-fascist Iron Front mark from the Timbers Army's support for gay identity. However, in the anti-identitarian Riveters, the combined symbols amplify their marginalized voices and represent a collective solidarity of difference empowered to fight back. As one Riveter explained,

> What the Iron Front represents, I feel like we're almost getting across with rainbow and we've been flying rainbow for seven years. We don't necessarily need Iron Front to send the message that rainbow is spreading. Creating that safe space inside the stadium, that welcoming thing, rainbow did that for us. People we put on stage did that for us. Visibility did that for us. When you're in a culture that's as vanilla as Timbers Army, you have to do things, I don't think the Riveters have to do that ... It was never a thing that we needed in order to prove that we were something. I hope that people just know that we are something and we don't have to wear a sign that says that we aren't.

The Riveters are anti-fascist because to not be would be to undermine their own community's strength. Queerness grounds the group's inclusion and will to fight fascist forces as not only a belief system but as necessary for survival. These survival needs predate the current political context, but the PTFC front office's default to corporatized neutrality by banning an anti-fascist symbol as "political," but allowing rainbow as a mark of inclusion at a time of rising violence against their community, heightened the stakes. For the Riveters, it was imperative to resist the culturally extractive work of the ban to assert the interconnection of queerness and anti-fascism as they came under threat.

Los Angeles: Diasporic Expressions

Los Angeles is the second largest city in the US and the city with the second highest percentage of foreign-born citizens. Not just Latin Americans, but the diaspora of groups from all over the world have made LA home, including but not limited to those from Korea, Japan, Greece, Germany, Ethiopia, Vietnam, Bangladesh, Russia, Guatemala, Poland, Nicaragua, and Armenia. Los Angeles' diversity shows up in the culture of soccer fandom in the city, and specifically within the stands of BMO Stadium. Dominated by subcultures from Mexico, Argentina, England and Germany, the diverse population of LA shows up as themselves to make the city's soccer culture a distinct phenomenon.

Supporters of a new football club in Los Angeles came together before LAFC even had a logo, manager, or players. As Chivas USA folded shortly before the announcement of LAFC, some fans were quick to support any team that was not the LA Galaxy. LAFC also provided previous Galaxy fans a new vision of local soccer to support in Los Angeles: a team within the city boundaries, near downtown and South Central LA. This articulation of localized identity quickly became the distinguishing quality of the supporters as well the club's promotional branding.

Supporter groups such as LAFC supporters Tigers, who are based in LA's Korea Town neighborhood, identify with their ethnic backgrounds as they support their soccer club. Additionally, Angel City FC supporter group Poderosas is a space for women of color to be fierce and show up unapologetically as those who may not be the traditional NWSL fan. These groups express their culture and fandom intersectionally. In the supporter sections, it is not uncommon to see supporters fly the flags of their diasporic origin or pride or trans flags to establish the space not just as passionate pro-LAFC or pro-ACFC, but as a space of inclusion.

For the White fanbase this becomes exciting, edgy, and fascinating, as the passion that LAFC's diverse supporters express is not found in many other places in American sports. However, for the mild, family friendly, upper middle and upper class of White Los Angeles, Angel City FC has in many ways succeeded in providing a space. Compared to LAFC matches, Angel City FC typically avoid weekday scheduling, and often schedule 5pm kickoffs for Saturday and Sunday night matches catering to the professional class family.

The White Spatial Imaginary of MLS & NWSL

MLS and NWSL engage in cultural extraction from fan subcultures in part because they are products of corporate efforts to capitalize on the youth soccer industry built in White American professional class suburban communities from the 1970s (Andrews, 2000; Allison, 2018). The leagues created teams that lacked rootedness in the immigrant and working class communities that maintained soccer prior to the White suburban embrace of the game. The wealthy founders of MLS and NWSL constructed team brands that aspired to homogenized neutrality grounded in what Lipsitz (2011: 29) calls "the white spatial imaginary." As he asserts whiteness is "not so much as a color as a condition" that leads White people, in this case, the people that run American professional soccer to create "'pure' and homogenous spaces, controlled environments, and predictable patterns of design and behavior [that] seek to hide social problems rather than solve them." Through the deployment of faux inclusionary marketing language that emphasized family-focused events the leagues imagined soccer stadiums as apolitical meritocratic spaces safe from the racialized and gendered inequality and discrimination that complicate everyday life. They envisioned the parents of White suburban soccer-playing children as their primary customers, even as they made uneven outreach to Latino/a/x communities (Delgado, 1999; Jensen and Sosa, 2008; Seese, 2014). The leagues located their identities in American whiteness, unnoticed by White culture, but hyper-visible to the ethnically marked soccer cultures it sought to replace.

The leagues targeted White suburban audiences raised on youth soccer in different ways: MLS centered a Eurocentric cosmopolitanism, while the women's leagues emphasized a postfeminist female empowerment. MLS targeted professional class White men who had become fans of European men's soccer to indicate their style differentiation from the wider population's interest in basketball and football. To signal authenticity to their imagined White audience, the league insisted on calling its franchises "clubs," even as they lacked historical roots in the athletic clubs that produced soccer teams in nineteenth-century Europe. Franchises adopted European naming conventions, eschewing the nicknames common in other sports for the terms United, Sporting, City, and Real. LAFC and Portland Timbers FC both include the term football in their name, avoiding soccer and specifically referencing the British name for the sport they play.

As MLS Europeanized their brand, women's soccer leagues in the early 2000s built on the narratives deployed in connection with the US women's national team to Americanize, heterosexualize, and feminize women's soccer to appeal to a similar audience of White professionals (Cole and Gardiana, 2013; Meân, 2015). Players were framed as wholesome gendered role models, the ultimate example of having a successful career while maintaining their role as mothers. In a postfeminist maneuver, women's professional soccer was sold to fans, media companies, and sponsors by reinforcing the notion that access was the sole structural barrier to achievement (Adjepong, 2017; McDonald, 2000).

NWSL's marketing centered White children, particularly the inspiration young girls could take away from seeing their heroes. This individualized empowerment-based outreach strategy followed what King (2004) calls the "market of generosity," in which consumers are urged to think they can make an impact on intractable social issues – like sexism, patriarchy, or misogynoir – through their purchases. In this case, spending money at a women's soccer match enables professional class fans to become "generous and civic-minded" citizens because they are financially supporting individual women's success within a patriarchal society. Linking families, role modeling and fandom created a stadium atmosphere shaped primarily by girls and their parents who expect wholesome entertainment. Players are expected to greet young fans after games and the resultant images are used in advertisements for future games. In both MLS and NWSL, targeting White professional class audiences eventually led to the leagues seeking a more diverse market, but only in ways that allowed them to keep their White spatial imaginary intact.

Extraction & Commodification

The incorporation of fan-generated culture into team brands was due in part to the recognition by the teams that the organized fan groups drive attendance. From their arrival in 2011, the Timbers Army helped Portland set the league standard for attendance with regular sellouts. In 2013, the Riveters did the same for the newly founded NWSL, earning an average attendance over 13,000 when no other franchise topped 4,500. Both groups feature prominently in PTFC marketing. The team's front office contains four photos, one of each team and one of each supporter group in action. In Los Angeles, teams are not only competing against other sporting events but also every other activity and attraction to get people in their stadium. In a city full of Hollywood, sunny beaches, and championship sports teams, the 3252 have been what sets LAFC apart. The supporter groups of LAFC show up every match day to cultivate an intense environment. The drums, singing, and smoke aren't only a way for fans to show their support, but it becomes currency for the marketing of these teams to show that their fans are authentic.

Ultimately, for LAFC and LA Galaxy, both fanbases and team popularity are driven in large part by LA's Latino/a/x population and their most efficient marketing tool has been the signings of star Mexican national team players. A history of talent such as Giovanni Jonathan Dos Santos, Chicharito, among others for Galaxy and Carlos Vela as the LAFC's first signing, are in large part what drive a diverse crowd to these games. With LAFC's quick gain of popularity in Los Angeles, LAFC established themselves as LA's true team and being situated closer to central and eastern LA, as the more Latino/a/x team.

Soccer brands also recognize that fan-generated culture helped authenticate their brands as inclusive. The soccer teams extract the identity-based elements of fan culture that can be more easily absorbed into their productive pursuits than the groups' collective structures and resistant politics. The resultant marketing campaigns and products contain an atomized version of fan subculture that includes recognizable symbols and images of fans, but also consciously avoids the more disruptive politics that produced the initial subculture. Instead of a diversity that celebrates and enhances the differences that make fan subculture meaningful to its practitioners, the leagues adopt slogans like "Soccer For All." that assimilate differences into a homogenized whole. Team and league marketing frame tifo displays, banners, and the release of colored smoke bombs as examples of extreme commitment to consumption-based fandom, rather than a distinct subculture. The leagues want the fan groups to be raucous, colorful, and fun, but not destabilizing and disruptive.

In 2019, PTFC opened a new grandstand with premium seating that overlooks performances of the Riveters and Timbers Army. The section includes a tribute wall with images of Timbers Army *tifos* and elevator bays painted with both groups' chant lyrics. The displays were created without the fan groups' permission or consultation, commodifying fan culture as something to be appreciated at a remove rather than a reflection of lived experience. On the day I toured the new stand, workers were painting over a section of the chant wall, because it said "What is the 107IST?" This phrase is not a chant, but rather the words listed at the bottom of the fan groups' gameday chant sheets. The wall designers had taken the words off the sheets without a thought to what the actual lyrics meant, extracting the culture and distancing it from the people who created and maintained it. As one Timbers Army member stated,

> It's no secret that the TA is the driving force in getting people to the stadium and we're proud of that. What we don't like is, just co-opting our culture. Them defining what that culture is and doing things without discussing it with us.

Or as a Riveter remarked, "At this point and time, the front office sees us as a money-making opportunity."

This work of extraction extends to the way PTFC includes rainbow in its brand. Importantly, none of the grandstand *tifo* photos includes Riveters pride displays or even any images of the Riveters. Instead of acknowledging the disruptive and community-building queerness at the heart of Thorns' fan culture, the team instead leans hard into respectability politics. Queerness is limited to homoliberal efforts that, "enfranchise straight-acting homosexuals at the expense of other unassimilable sexual minorities" (Warner, 2012: xi). PTFC turns franchise logos rainbow for a month in June, stressing empowerment through consumption with corporate-branded Pride events and their associated rainbow-themed merchandise. PTFC persists with homoliberal appeals, even as it puts off some Riveters, As one argued,

> They're marketing to the wrong people. The people with all the money are the queers that are buying all the beers and buying all the merch and loving this inclusive space and being able to be themselves and chant and sing and dance and yell and scream and heckle.

PTFC's appeal to dollars stresses a vague openness, appearing inclusive enough to maintain non-normative fans and their allies as consumers (McDonald, 2008), but making no fundamental shifts in definitions of who can and should be a fan or taking action to thwart legislative and material threats to queer lives.

At the core of LAFC's supporter culture is its diversity. In contrast to suburban Carson, California's Los Angeles Galaxy, one of MLS's inaugural teams, LAFC markets itself as the inner city and Brown team. As the chants rock through BMO stadium in Spanish, their branding is noticeable. LAFC often use the taglines, "in the Heart of LA," "Shoulder to shoulder," "Uniting the world's city through the world's game" to indicate that they have penetrated the streets of LA as the city's true team, while simultaneously creating a club that has become hostile to the city's working class which includes many Latino/a/x locals. Recently LAFC has boasted of its one billion dollar valuation via Forbes and ticket prices on the resale market regularly price fans out as the second highest cost in MLS (Birnbaum, 2023; Myers, 2022).

In order to capitalize on the diversity of the teams and to extract the authenticity of the cultural performance in the stands while also attempting to emphasize their surface level commitment to diversity, both Angel City FC and LAFC regularly host theme matches of Asian-American Pacific Islander Nights, Latin American culture, while seldom recognizing the diversity and cultural differences within these unique groups and their larger role in the community.

Policing & Resistance

As the bans show, the process of cultural extraction includes policing. Even as leagues and teams attempt to take ownership of fan culture by incorporating images of fan-generated spectacle, they police subcultural performances that stray too far from encouraging people to purchase the spectacular product. Anything that cannot be neutralized and homogenized into their unmarked professional class (White) brand is deemed "political" and thus impinging upon the pleasure and escapism of sports. The risk of restraining fan subculture to suit marketing is that both the marginalized people who have done the labor to create the culture and political actors who actively seek to undermine and destroy it, recognize the shallowness of the brands' engagement. Regressive organizations target branded merchandise and theme nights for high visibility protest, while the organized fan groups reinterpret their battles with team management to strengthen their subcultural community and further political organizing.

Portland: There Is No Middle Ground

MLS banned the Iron Front mark before the 2019 season ostensibly for its associations with a political organization they labeled ANTIFA.[1] When fans in Portland and elsewhere protested, MLS issued a release stating,

> We and our clubs will continue to permit signs that support basic human rights, as the rainbow pride flag does, as well as those that condemn racism and fascism. The prohibition on political signage is in place to support the overwhelming majority of MLS fans who come to our stadiums to enjoy a great soccer game.

The statement engages in cultural extraction because it at once neutralizes the rainbow flag as apolitical and asserts that the "overwhelming majority" of fans seek a depoliticized stadium grounded in whiteness, where they do not need to consider the "politics" of inequality.

The ban, particularly the move to extend it to NWSL games not governed by MLS, spurred the Riveters alongside the Timbers Army into a series of creative acts to amplify the symbol, its political significance, and links between anti-fascism and radical queerness. The night before the home opener for both teams, the Riveters organized a stenciling party at a printing studio. Patches, bags, and t-shirts were marked with the Iron Front using bleach, paint, and dye. On gameday, fans snuck in the apparel and integrated it into a noticeable number of other anti-fascist shirts, scarves, and banners, particularly among the highly visible *capos* and drummers, a gender diverse group that includes trans, genderqueer, and cis people. For the Riveters opening day, one *capo* wore a sparkly new hat with a unicorn and another tested out new shoes in the trans pride stripes of light blue, pink, and white. At the start of the match, *capo* Sunday White, grabbed Gloria the giant rainbow flag, and swung it back and forth, as if on the bow of a ship trying to signal someone on shore. Her hair was raised in six spikes, one each for a different color of the rainbow. During the national anthem, the *capos* remained still, the drummers sat, and some Riveters turned their backs on the field. The Riveters are always active, but this day felt a bit more aggressive. The message could not have been clearer: We're here, we're back, and no one is going to tell what we can wear, what we can do, and more than anything, anti-fascism means that difference and vulnerability, particularly queer difference and vulnerability, are welcome here. Racism, homophobia, and hate are not.

In the face of team management's maneuvers to uncouple the rainbow flag from anti-fascism, the Riveters maintained their space as decidedly the opposite. Their actions – the DIY creation of Iron Front gear and then sneaking it into the stadium; the collective decision by the *capos* and drummers to not participate in the national anthem, and the semi-organized choice to wear clothing with anti-fascist messages – set out to disrupt the front office's seemingly benign, but ultimately dangerous, prohibition of political speech. Taken together the embodied actions reflect the Riveters' ingenuity in using their stadium platform to reclaim their culture. The Iron Front activism took place, not as an extra obligation or one-off display but was integrated into the cultural labors already at work.

From this start, the Portland fan groups saturated the North End with the Iron Front symbol for the summer's duration and strategically amplified other performances of anti-fascism to reclaim their culture. At a time when White supremacists repeatedly targeted Portland, the Riveters changed a lyric of the chant, *Oh When the Thorns Go Marching In* from the usual "Fuck [the opposition team's city]" refrain to "Fuck the Nazis," the refrain unmistakably audible on the broadcast. At another match, the Riveters loudly rebuked Donald Trump, booing as the line "that I will obey the orders of the President of the United States" was read over the public address during a halftime swearing-in ceremony for military cadets. Sunday White consistently conducted chants in an Iron Front dress, while a marked banner behind the home goal appeared regularly on television (Figure 7.4). The Timbers Army turned the Portlandia Iron Front banner into a shirt with the words 'No Pasarán' (They Shall Not Pass), a phrase originally sung by anti-Franco forces during the Spanish Civil War and now used globally by socialist and anti-fascist organizations and activists.

As the campaign built and spread to other MLS and NWSL groups, the Portland groups took the step of redrawing the fan-generated spectacle craved by the leagues for an August weekend. On Friday, the Timbers Army and Seattle's Emerald City Supporters remained silent for the first 33 minutes of the match to mark the year that the Nazis banned the Iron Front. Two days later, the Riveters paid tribute to the White Rose, another 1940s anti-Nazi group, by covering the section in white roses and fronting their section with four large banners with the messages: Silence = Complicity; Which Side Are You On; If You're Not Anti, You're Pro, There is No Middle Ground; and the Elie Weisel quote, "We must take sides. Neutrality helps the oppressor, never the victim" (Figures 7.5–7.7). They replaced their colorful player tribute banners with greyscale banners that addressed the ban and its misapplication to Thorns

Figure 7.4 Sunday White in Iron Front Dress, August 11, 2019. Photo by Darren Lloyd/107IST.

games. These banners appeared for two matches, their colorless presence expressly removing the rainbow. By mid-season, the confrontation had drawn national attention and by the end of the year, MLS rescinded the ban.

The stated purpose of the ban was to on one hand allow fans to enjoy a depoliticized sports environment, while on the other incorporate some parts of fan subculture like the rainbow flag into the dominant stadium environment. The work of the Portland fan groups shows the limits and ultimate weaknesses of extractive culture. They were able to repoliticize the rainbow flag by making explicit connections to the banned symbol, while also amplifying the provocative anti-fascist politics of the Iron Front. They successfully sutured MLS's actions to the more distasteful politics of White supremacy and Nazism, overcoming the ban and creating a strengthened space for further anti-fascist and queer organizing.

Los Angeles: Pride Republic and the Puto Chant

With the culturally diverse fan base in Los Angeles, there becomes a diversity of political thought and propensity toward inclusivity. With a growing xenophobic rhetoric, reignited by the Trump era, the "Puto chant" became associated with Latino/a/x fans, and with recent events at the 2023 CONCACAF Gold Cup, where a select number fans during Mexican national team matches have been engaging in physical altercations, Latino/a/x fans all together have been stereotyped as homophobic, intolerant, and violent. While

94 Chris W. Henderson and Pratik Nyaupane

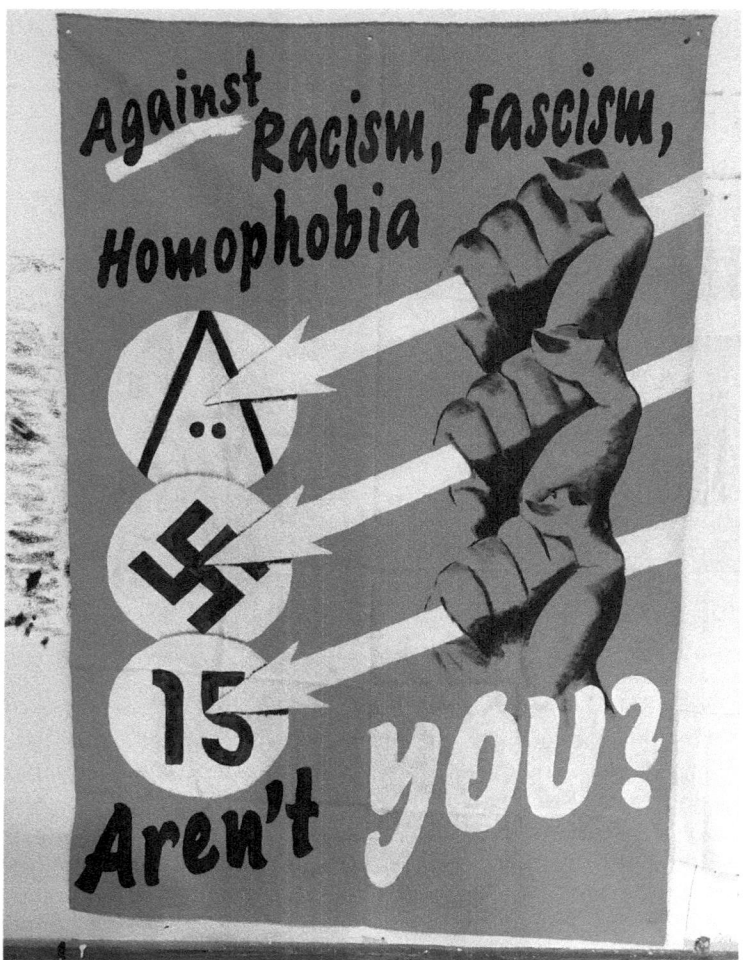

Figure 7.5 If You're Not Anti, You're Pro Banner, Portland, August 2019. Image courtesy of Holly Duthie.

the homophobic chant has been of concern in Los Angeles, the team and the 3252 have made an effort to counter any forms of homophobia and transphobia. Pride Republic are a supporter group of LGBTQ+ LAFC supporters who seek the stands of BMO Stadium as a space for them to be themselves and free from homophobia. A majority of fans and the 3252 vehemently opposed these intolerant chants, but as the team has an image to fix, they have chosen to extract and utilize the Pride Republic's membership. During pre-match ceremonies each of the official supporter groups fly their flags, in addition to two pride flags, in an attempt to portray inclusivity. With the 3252 consisting of many members that belong to the LGBTQ+ community, they have made it

Figure 7.6 Greyscale Against Racism, Fascism, Homophobia Banner, Portland, August 2019. Image courtesy of Holly Duthie.

clear that they stand against homophobia. The supporter groups seem to support the club's crackdown on the puto chant.

Ultimately, the Puto chant has been a stain on many Latino/a/x fans in the US, while only a select few engage with the behavior. The stereotype that Latino/a/x fans are aggressive, loud, and violent makes for great promotional material for MLS to show that soccer is popular and has authentic fans in the US, but only as long as they get to control how these diverse audiences show up and

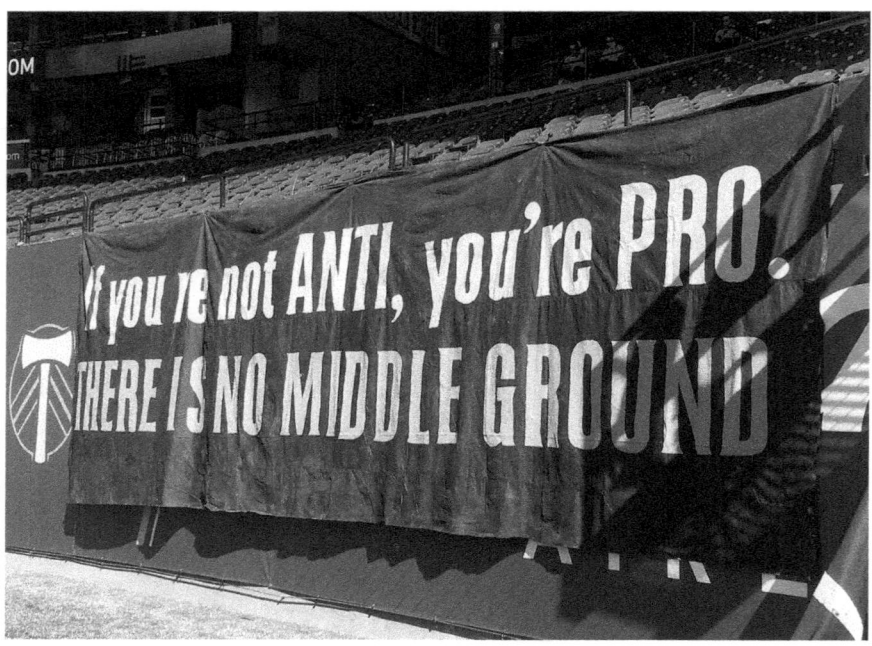

Figure 7.7 Greyscale Against Hand Me Down Blues Banner, Portland, August 2019. Image courtesy of Holly Duthie.

engage within the stadium. When LAFC play against their cross town rivals LA Galaxy, it becomes a spectacle of culture, fan authenticity, and football, but also two passionate fan bases that occasionally conflict. As a way to combat violence during the LA derby match (also called El Tráfico, a pun on el clásico and LA's infamous traffic) there is always increased police presence, heightened security, and an effort to physically separate opposing fan groups. Notably, as stadium announcements and team press statements are often in English, these calls to end violence are always emphasized in Spanish as a targeted message. In April of 2022, in the wake of violent incidents between the two LA men's clubs and a tragic brawl in Queretaro, Mexico where several fans were killed and many more injured, the two team's released a joint video and statement in English and Spanish to call for peace and no violence between the supporters (Jalón, 2022). While the violence has stained the occassions in which these two teams play, it has also become a worry for MLS and these teams as they want the authentic Latin American and European "feel" of soccer without the negative consequences that passionate fandom often can lead to.

Conclusion: The Challenges of Extractive Culture

Identifying and articulating cultural extraction illuminates one way that the uneven and unequal struggle over and through popular culture, takes place in the current sociopolitical environment. As hyper-partisanship manifests simultaneously with capital's infiltration of even the most marginal of subcultures, the meaning, practice, and ultimately the power of cultural practice remains contested. Foregrounding cultural extraction shows that many of the current contestations are localized confrontations with particular conditions. Marginalized people can – and sometimes do – find ways to assert collective power to maintain their subcultural communities, even as capital seeks to carve them up into easily digestible and monetized bits.

Extractive culture is a potentially powerful tool for dominant institutions in the ideological and material struggles that take place through popular culture. However, the practice is ultimately vulnerable to countermeasures from subcultural creators. This is particularly true, as is the case with American professional soccer, when the institutions seek to depoliticize subculture by limiting its symbols to an identity-based inclusion. A significant part of what gives queer and Latino/a/x soccer subculture meaning and power is the way in which the people who create it use it to build connections with each other and sustain themselves in the face of marginalization. Therefore when the soccer brands attempt to extract something that does not belong to them for the purpose of advertising depoliticized spectacle they find themselves challenged by the very people they seek to include. This leaves their inclusionary campaigns hollow and more easily undone both by the organized fan culture, but also more regressive political actors who police, sometimes violently, any activity by mainstream institutions that engages in tolerance. If institutions like MLS and NWSL are to move away from their origins in professional class White culture to a more diverse place, they will need to engage more deeply at a political level with the fan-generated culture than the current extractive model.

Note

1 Although some local anti-fascist organizations adopt names like Rose City Antifa. There is no political organization named ANTIFA. The term is commonly used among anti-fascists as shorthand for anti-fascist.

References

Adjepong, A (2017) 'We're, like, a cute rugby team': How whiteness and heterosexuality shape women's sense of belonging in rugby. *International Review for the Sociology of Sport* 52(2), 209–222.
Allison, R (2018) *Kicking Center: Gender and the Selling of Women's Professional Soccer*. New Brunswick, NJ. Rutgers University Press.
Andrews, D L (2000) Contextualizing suburban soccer: Consumer culture, lifestyle differentiation, and suburban America. *Culture, Sport, Society* 2(3), 31–53.
Bailey, M (2013) *Butch Queens Up in Pumps: Gender Performance and Ballroom Culture in Detroit*. Ann Arbor. University of Michigan Press.
Balta, V (18 June 2018). 'Homophobic and not very clever': Why puto chants haunt Mexican football. *The Guardian*. https://www.theguardian.com/football/2018/jun/18/puto-chants-mexico-football-world-cup. (Accessed: 13 June 2023).

Birnbaum, J (2023, 2 February). Major League Soccer's most valuable clubs 2023: LAFC is the first billion-dollar franchise. *Forbes*. https://www.forbes.com/sites/justinbirnbaum/2023/02/02/major-league-soccers-most-valuable-clubs-2023-lafc-is-the-first-billion-dollar-franchise/?sh=7b5013a65324 (Accessed: 27 August 2023).

Cole, C L & Giardina, M D (2013) Embodying American democracy: Performing the female sporting icon. In: Andrews, D L and Carrington, B (eds) *Blackwell Companions in Cultural Studies: A Companion to Sport (1)*. Somerset. Wiley-Blackwell, pp. 532–547.

Conquergood, D (2013) *Cultural Struggles: Performance, Ethnography, Praxis*. In: Johnson, EP (ed). Ann Arbor. The University of Michigan Press. Available from: https://press.umich.edu/Books/C/Cultural-Struggles2

Delgado, F (1999) Sport and politics: Major League Soccer, constitution, and (the) Latino audience(s). *Journal of Sport and Social Issues* 23(1), 41–54.

Dolan, J (2012) *The Feminist Spectator as Critic*, 2nd ed. Ann Arbor. University of Michigan Press.

Hall, S (1981) Notes on deconstructing "the popular." In Samuel, R (ed) *People's History and Socialist Theory*. London. Routledge, pp. 227–240.

Hebdige, D (1979) *Subculture: The Meaning of Style*. London. Routledge.

Henderson, C W (2015) Two balls is too many: Stadium performance and queerness among Portland's Rose City Riveters supporters club. *Sport in Society* 21(7), 1031–1046.

Jalón, R (2022, 7 April) LAFC and LA Galaxy supporter groups reflect on violence and respecting each other before 'El Tràfico'. *L.A. Taco*. https://lataco.com/lafc-galaxy-violence-trafico-rivalry (Accessed: 27 August 2023).

Jensen, R & Sosa, J (2008) The importance of building positive relationships between Hispanic audiences and Major League Soccer franchises: A case study of the public relations challenges facing Houston 1836. *Soccer & Society* 9(4), 477–490.

Kelley, R D G (1997). *Yo' Mama's disfunktional*. Boston, MA. Beacon Press.

King, S (2004) Pink Ribbons Inc: Breast cancer activism and the politics of philanthropy. *International Journal of Qualitative Studies in Education* 17(4), 473–492.

Kuhn, G (2011) *Soccer vs. the State*. Oakland, CA. PM Press.

Lee, C (2022) *The Defiant: A History of Football against Fascism*. Chichester. Pitch Publishing.

Lipsitz, G (2011) *How Racism Takes Place*. Philadelphia, PA. Temple University Press.

Madison, D S (2010) *Acts of Activism: Human Rights as Radical Performance*. Cambridge. Cambridge University Press.

Madison, D S (2011) *Critical ETHNOGRAPHY: Method, ETHICS, and Performance*, 2nd edition. Thousand Oaks, CA. Sage Publications.

McDonald, M (2000) The marketing of the Women's National Basketball Association and the making of postfeminism. *International Review for the Sociology of Sport* 35(1), 35–47.

McDonald, M (2008). Rethinking resistance: The queer play of the Women's National Basketball Association, visibility politics and late capitalism. *Leisure Studies* 27(1), 77–93.

Meân, L (2015) The 99ers: Celebrating the mythological. *Journal of Sport Media* 10(2), 31–43.

Muñoz, J E (1999) *Disidentifications: Queers of Color and the Performance of Politics*. Minneapolis. University of Minnesota Press.

Myers, J (25 July 2022). Analysis: Where Crew ticket prices rank in MLS; why 2023 season-ticket prices are changing. *The Columbus Dispatch*. https://www.dispatch.

com/story/sports/mls/columbus-crew/2022/07/25/why-columbus-crew-lowering-season-ticket-prices-many-sections-mls/10100167002/?utm_campaign=snd-autopilot (Accessed: 27 August 2023).

Peña, E A (2011) *Performing Piety: Making Space Sacred with the Virgin of Guadalupe*. Berkeley. University of California Press.

Seese, D (2014) New traditionalists: The emergence of modern America and the birth of the MLS coalition. In: Kiuchi, Y (ed) *Soccer Culture in America: Essays on the World's Sport in Red, White, and Blue*. Jefferson, NC. McFarland & Company, Inc., pp. 43–68.

Taylor, D (2003). *The Archive and the Repertoire: Performing Cultural Memory in the Americas*. Durham, NC. Duke University Press.

Thompson, F (16 September 2019). Sounders supporters meet with team after leader ejected for Iron Front flag. *Q13 Fox KCPQ*. https://www.fox13seattle.com/news/sounders-supporters-meet-with-team-after-leader-ejected-for-iron-front-flag (Accessed: 27 August 2023).

Velez, J (1 May 2018) New L.A. Soccer team already dealing with fans chanting 'P*to' at inaugural game — fun or offensive? *L.A. Taco*. https://lataco.com/new-l-a-soccer-team-already-dealing-with-fans-chanting-pto-at-inaugural-game-fun-or-offensive (Accessed: 27 August 2023).

Warner, S (2012) *Acts of Gaiety: LGBT Performance and the Politics of Pleasure*. Ann Arbor. University of Michigan Press.

8 Resistance, Opposition, and Campaigns
Extending the 'Fan-Opticon'

Mark Turner and Jan Andre Lee Ludvigsen

Introduction

As we argued in Chapter 1, a number of critical events (perhaps most notably the *Stade de France* 2022 Champions League final, the Euro 2020 final) along with other changes to the regulation of football fans (e.g., the introduction of 'Safe Standing'; Baroness Casey's review into the events at Euro 2020) mean that we could critically approach the current epoch as a critical juncture – characterized by large-scale changes that give life to an enduring legacy (cf. Della Porta, 2020) – in terms of social control in football. Beyond academic spheres (Pearson and Stott, 2022; Lee Ludvigsen, 2023; Silverstone and Lee Ludvigsen, 2022), questions surrounding the future of fans' safety have also been asked by fan representatives, politicians, and the media, including a *BBC Panorama* documentary investigating what went wrong at the 2022 Champions League final, which screened in October 2022.

Against this background, marked by a (social) football world in flux, this chapter aims to constructively develop our (neo-)Foucauldian concept – the 'fan-opticon' – which in broad terms captures how football fans are considered by football and political authorities to be potential threats to the 'natural order' that is desired within football stadiums and spaces (Turner and Lee Ludvigsen, 2023). As we unpack later, we originally advanced this concept in context of English football where we analysed historical and more recent developments within the field of 'Safe Standing'; including the announcement that confirmed that so-called 'licensed Safe Standing' would be approved for use in English football before the 2022/2023 season subject to strict surveillance and crowd control conditions (ibid.). The discourses surrounding the reintroduction of standing inside English and Welsh football stadia for the first time since 1994, hence, were marked by discourses suggesting that standing – even when deemed to be 'safe' and 'licensed' – still represented a potential nuisance to the desired, ordered, and pacified spaces within the football stadium (ibid.).

However, as we demonstrate in this chapter, our 'fan-opticon' concept can also be applied to other football contexts, and international sport mega-events.

DOI: 10.4324/9781003453062-8

In particular, our purpose is to utilize some contemporary exemplars to examine here the ways in which fans perform and express what Foucault (2008) called 'counter-conduct' to resist a selection of the disciplining mechanisms firmly situated within the 'fan-opticon' of government. In order to do so, this chapter builds on our previous, co-authored, and single authored work into safety, security, social movements and contestations in football (e.g., Turner, 2017, 2021, 2023; Lee Ludvigsen, 2022a, 2022b, 2023a, 2023b). We also draw from extant literatures and media sources to identify exemplars across different European settings speaking to how modes of resistance and opposition, since the 1980s, have emerged *alongside* football's security and surveillance cultures.

Conceptual Touchstones: Extending the 'Fan-Opticon'

As displayed throughout this edited collection's various chapters, and the earlier literature (e.g., Tsoukala, 2008; Kossakowski et al., 2020; Lee Ludvigsen, 2022a) social control mechanisms in football both typically and broadly target football fans. As Pearson (1999) observed in the late 1990s, exceptional social control measures such as football banning orders, alcohol bans, enhanced surveillance, and intelligence collection are often seen as 'legitimate' if deployed in football contexts. Indeed, draconian social control mechanisms 'against citizens who chose to spend their Saturdays watching football matches, rather than going shopping or attending other kinds of sporting events can often be seen as essential and desirable' (p. 28). Indeed, very few other sports themselves are subject to the same social control and policing measures as football.

Such social and legislative trends, importantly, are evident across a myriad of European contexts in the current day but can undoubtedly be traced historically as Tsoukala et al.'s (2016) authoritative analysis demonstrates. Indeed, historically, but particularly from the 1980s and onwards, the (often) unnuanced political and media consensus that football fans are 'social enemies' (Tsoukala, 2008) have contributed both to the criminalization of football fandom and cultures, as well as the securitization of fans (whereby fans are discursively presented as security threats) (see Lee Ludvigsen, 2023; May, 2015). The effectiveness of social control mechanisms implemented in football, however, remains highly contested and, in some cases, they have proved counter-productive (e.g., Pearson and Sale, 2011; Pearson and Stott, 2022).

Notwithstanding, because elite football has opened itself up for sociological and criminological analyses of risk, security, safety, regulation, and social control, so have social scientists turned towards Michel Foucault's body of work in attempts to make sense of these trends (Lee Ludvigsen, 2022b). Given this chapter's short nature, this is not the place for an extended account of Foucault's (1977, 1978, 2008) seminal ideas on 'power', 'government' and 'discipline'. Notwithstanding, to understand the 'fan-opticon', a brief account of Foucault's panopticon is necessary.

At the heart of Foucault's (1977) governmentality project were the ideas that disciplinary and increasingly subtle modes of power had taken over for earlier types of sovereign and coercively articulated modes of power. These new modes of power targeted individuals and groups and this shift predominantly took place from the eighteenth century and onwards. Importantly, for Foucault, English philosopher Jeremy Bentham's panopticon prison model – designed so that a single guard located in a watchtower could watch all the prisoners without the prisoners' knowledge – came to represent the modern society for Foucault. Here, the state with its technologies, discourses, architectures, and *dispositifs* surveilled or monitored its citizens who then had to assume that they are being watched. This, in turn, served to regulate citizens' behaviour (Foucault, 1977).

A series of critical extensions of the 'panopticon' exist. This includes Bigo's (2006) 'ban-opticon' which examines how the concentrated surveillance of a *selected few* (rather than everyone) became normalized in the fields of European immigration and security in the 2000s. Transporting these concepts (Bigo, 2006; Foucault, 1977) into the world of football, we thus introduced the 'fan-opticon' to capture how the football stadium, as a whole, can be approached through a panoptic lens, and specifically, how so-called 'licensed standing areas' within the stadium, become characterized by concentrated surveillance of a minority of fans that stand inside the ground:

> as [a] *dispositif* and driver behind the evolving securitization of football-related milieus. It can be defined as the relational mechanisms and discursive vectors that collectively discipline football fans and particularly a targeted minority that are considered to destabilize the 'natural order' within football stadia. These mechanisms encompass the social, spatial but also temporal elements that contribute towards, and contest, the normalized surveillant regime in the football world which regulate and constrain the ritual of watching football. *Notwithstanding, the concept also captures and recognizes the networks of resistance and counter-power that co-exist alongside authorities, football's regulatory bodies and clubs' attempts to discipline fans.*
> (Turner and Lee Ludvigsen, 2023: 11, emphasis added)

However, there are two points that we wish to make, rationalizing why we seek to unpack our concept further, and reflect on its potential transportability. First, as discussed, we exploratorily advanced the concept in the case study of English football and the 'Safe Standing' developments between 1988 and 2022 (for a full social history of this movement, see Turner, 2023). As such, locating the 'fan-optic' mechanisms in other, transnational contexts remains imperative for the sociological make-up of a more comparative study. Second, and most crucial here, we were originally not able to examine, describe, and analyse in full how resistance networks and fans' 'counter-power' were expressed beyond the article's context (Turner and Lee Ludvigsen, 2023).

Hence, we proceed to describe and discuss at greater length here the 'counter-power' and 'counter-conduct' that emerge within different fan cultures in Europe through collective actions that seek to challenge the criminalization of football fandom and securitization of football spaces. This therefore assists the aim of, specifically, developing our understanding of fans' 'counter-power' and 'counter-conduct', and how supporters' resist the governmentality of political and football authorities' policies, technologies, and discourses.

Protest, Resistance, and Campaigns

In a European football context, this section throws a light on how some football fan groups resist, protest or oppose diverse social control mechanisms. We do so by using historical and more recent examples. To fully understand fans' modes of contestation, however, a short unpacking of fans' political activism, engagement, and collective is required, given their position as a growing field in mainstream sociology and the sociologies of sport and social movements (e.g., Millward, 2011; Hill et al., 2018; Cleland et al., 2018; Kossakowski et al., 2020; Turner, 2023).

To begin with, it is necessary to critically approach football as a *social (life-)world*. This lifeworld consists of networked configurations of players, agents, fans, administrators, journalists, politicians, law enforcers, owners, and other *social actors* that have diverse interests in the sport and possess different levels of power (Cleland et al., 2018). Within this social world, we argue, supporters are important stakeholders (Lee Ludvigsen, 2022a; Turner, 2021, 2023) who occasionally choose to engage politically and campaign against a variety of issues largely caused by neoliberal forces in the sport. For instance, high ticket prices, the exclusion of 'traditional' fans, the formation of 'break-away' leagues such as the 'European Super League', and Safe Standing (Cleland et al., 2018; Turner and Millward, 2023; Turner, 2023).[1] Thus, as Kossakowski et al. (2020) write, the existing library of studies on the fans-politics nexus can be divided into to three fields. First, researchers have increasingly explored the general political commitment of supporters. Second, other scholars examine single political issues (e.g., nationalism, racism, identity, homophobia, legal restrictions) via analyses of fandom. Finally, we may observe that analysts have explored how we may read political incidents such as protests or revolutions through the lens of football fans and their civic activities.

It is within the second field we situate fans' resistance against security and safety regimes in football. However, in comparison to analyses concentrating on how fans are governed, less attention has, specifically, been dedicated to how governmentality rationales of social control targeting football fans have been actively contested and even led to formal opposition or resistance. This, despite the fact that '[s]upporters are more and more controlled and disciplined and have less freedom to set their own behavioural tolerance levels' (Spaaij, 2013: 179). At the same time, while these contestations may appear particularly focused on football-specific legislation, regulation, or policing practices, it is important to highlight that they, in some cases, also are directed towards broader societal concerns. For example, questions about the security measures' impact on urban cultures, spaces, the social freedoms of supporters (Giulianotti, 2011), and civil liberties.

Since the 1980s, football fans across different European contexts have resisted technological and legislative imperatives in football and authorities' and leagues' discourses seeking to regulate their behaviours, activities, or cultures. These imperatives have conserved the 'common knowledge' (cf. Pearson, 1999) on football fans as (potential) 'threats' to the social and public order. Moreover, in different national contexts, we can observe how political elites have clashed with, or clamped down on fan groups. Perhaps most notably, and at different times, both Margaret Thatcher and Donald Tusk waged a 'war on hooliganism' in the UK and Poland respectively (Kossakowski et al., 2020). Naturally, while non-uniform, exceptional and everyday governmentality discourses and decisions have been critically reflected upon by various fan groups.

While one early fan response to being presented as social villains in the 1980s was the emergence of football fanzines movements (Giulianotti, 1999), it is important to highlight that such responses have spread across Europe and taken up new shapes. As Numerato states:

> Fans commonly questioned their criminalisation in public debate and resisted the perspective of fans as 'potential troublemakers'. As some fans put it, and repeatedly reiterated during public forums 'if you treat supporters like animals they will act like animals' [...] Furthermore, some fans criticised inadequate and excessive security measures, notably when applied to social groups who apparently do not represent any threat to public order, such as children, retired fans, or pregnant women. As an English fan critically engaged with security measures highlighted, police 'cannot impose these draconian measures to ordinary fans'.
>
> (Numerato, 2018: 15)

Football Fans and 'Counter-Conduct'

In the remainder of this chapter, we explore some of these acts of resistance or opposition through ideas of 'counter-power' and 'counter-conduct'. As such, we argue that while clubs, leagues, football authorities, political bodies, and the police are commonly considered as the most powerful actors in football's safety and security field – as those actors who dictate the security field (Lee Ludvigsen, 2023b) and the 'common knowledge' on football fans (cf. Pearson, 1999) – some fans actively counter this through formal and informal channels. Michel Foucault (1978: 95–96) famously observed that: 'Where there is power, there is resistance, and yet, or rather consequently, this resistance is never in a position of exteriority in relation to power'. Indeed, the Foucauldian

mechanisms of government are therefore commonly interwoven with dissenting 'counter-conducts' and so, power and resistance remain intrinsically connected (Spaaij, 2013; Rosol, 2014).

The idea of 'counter-conduct' was introduced by Foucault (2008) in *Security, Territory and Population: Lectures at the College de France 1977–1978*. Here, he defined it as a 'struggle against the processes implemented for conducting others' (p. 201). As he noted, the question of 'counter-conduct' remained important because question of how to govern – throughout the fifteenth and sixteenth centuries – were also followed by questions of how *not to be* governed (Odysseos et al., 2016). In that sense, 'counter-conduct' came to capture the 'resistance to processes of governmentality, as distinct from political revolts against sovereignty or material revolts against economic exploitation' (Death, 2016: 209). Thus, 'counter-conduct' are subdued and diffuse types of resistance and, as Rosol (2014: 71) writes, it 'more adequately captures certain forms of contestation in urban politics that go beyond open protest or direct confrontation'. As with the 'counter-conduct' concept as a whole, it has remained under-developed in the study of sport, fandom, and social movements (perhaps explained by the fact that Foucault did not elaborate much upon it [see Rosol, 2014]). Thus, in relation to sport and football, most specifically, we seek to provide a few examples below. These examples serve primarily three purposes. First, they serve to show how networks of counter-power and resistance co-exist alongside those actors that discipline football fans (cf. Turner and Lee Ludvigsen, 2023). Second, they suggest the *types* of issues that fans react to within this chapter's context. Finally, we merely provide brief snapshots of these 'mini cases'. Thus, these are all examples that require more detailed, empirical research as we are unable to yield an exhaustive account here for reasons of brevity.

While fans express their discontent with what they perceive as strict regulations and laws in both 'offline' and 'online' settings, through fanzines, message boards, podcasts, banners, and pop-up protests (Lee Ludvigsen, 2022b, 2023a), we may also identify specific campaigns that emerge in a response to the regulation of supporters. In England and Wales, one primary example is the Football Supporters Association's (FSA) 'Watching Football is not a Crime' campaign which has united supporters from different rival clubs (Turner, 2017). As argued elsewhere, this campaign has sought to ensure that fans are policed fairly and to place a spotlight on fans' rights. Yet, it remains important to note that as part of this campaign, the FSA also joined forced with the civil rights organization, Liberty, in order to challenge the decision to detain 80 Stoke City fans from a pub in Manchester in 2008 (Lee Ludvigsen, 2023). In this case, FSA (which was then named FSF), Liberty and Stoke City challenged the legitimacy of this action, and their campaigning led to fans being financially compensated and an apology being issued to the fans (Giulianotti, 2011). Yet, across Europe, too, as Numerato (2018: 16) writes, the suggestion that 'Watching Football is not a Crime' remains a 'well-known slogan'; and examples of fans' resisting policies or legislation that serve to either discipline or criminalize fans or their cultures – such as supporter identification cards – can be found in the contexts of Czech (ibid.), Italian (Testa, 2018), Polish (Kossakowski et al., 2020), Sweden (Carlsson and Backman, 2023), and Danish football (Joern, 2009), to name a few.

It is therefore important to highlight that, in certain cases, fans' resistance or opposition to security and safety policies are responsive to issues emerging within the course of a season, or for a specific fixture. Meanwhile, in other cases, they relate or speak wider public, security-related debates. Concerning the former, one recent example of this can be identified in the case of Feyenoord's away game against Roma in April 2023 for the UEFA Europa League quarter finals. Here, Italian authorities first banned Roma from selling tickets to Feyenoord fans due to historical incidents of disorder. UEFA then instructed Feyenoord not to sell tickets to Roma supporters for the first leg in Rotterdam (BBC, 2023). In various fan communities, these decisions were actively opposed and seen as decisions based on the criminalization of football fans and the view of football supporters as 'troublemakers. In a statement titled 'Stop Criminalising Football Supporters', the Feyenoord fan group *De Feijenoorder* (2023) challenged these decisions and highlighted the lack of dialogue with fans in the decision-making, and the repressive nature of the decision to exclude away fans. The statement concluded with: 'Do not ruin football: Stop Criminalising Football Supporters'.

Concerning the latter, we can look towards the impact of increasingly pre-emptive surveillance techniques on modern societies. Consequently, civil liberty and privacy concerns have proliferated both externally and internally to sport (Fussey and Sandhu, 2022). In this context, we see examples of how fan movements are in interaction with other social movements, seeking to mobilize campaigns on citizenship, rights, democracy, and liberty. Here, it is worth pointing out how, for example, the European-wide football fan network, Football Supporters Europe (2022), called on the European Parliament to protect citizens from biometric mass surveillance techniques and thereby joined a global coalition of 53 civil society organizations who called on EU lawmakers. In football, the deployment (and planned deployment) of such technologies have, in recent years, been heavily criticized by fan groups and civil liberty groups alike (The Guardian, 2019) and in 2019, *BBC* (2019) reported that '[a] fans' group asked supporters to wear Halloween masks to the south Wales football derby in protest at the use of facial recognition technology'.[2] What remains important to mention in this regard is that, within the sporting world, these debates are likely to continue and take new turns among supporter groups and anti-Olympic movements. Especially following the recent decision in France (in March 2023) to approve the use of Artificial Intelligence surveillance to secure the 2024 Summer Olympics in Paris in which football features as one of the sports. This, despite opposition from Amnesty International and other digital rights groups over the potential threat such technologies pose to citizens' civil liberties (Foroudi, 2023). As an Amnesty International (2023) statement asserted:

> This colossal surveillance architecture, according to French lawmakers, is 'experimental' and will be used to ensure safety and security during

the games. Amnesty International fears, however, that this bill will expand police powers by broadening the government's arsenal of surveillance equipment, permanently.

This, again, raises questions about the normalization of surveillance cultures *via* sport which Amnesty International's Secretary General, Agnes Callamard also commented on: 'We must ask ourselves some urgent questions: Who sets the norm for what is "normal"?' (quoted in Amnesty International, 2023). Moreover, two important questions here speak to, first, how supporters' and fan networks' contestations may align with, and become integrated with those of wider social movements or non-governmental organizations. Second, and with reference to the 'fan-opticon', given football stadiums and sport mega-events' historical and contemporary position as socio-spatial 'testing grounds' for surveillance technology and security measures (Lee Ludvigsen, 2022a), we argue that it is possible to examine potential synergies between football fan networks and networks of anti-Olympic activists who broadly critique the militarization and policing practices that follow every Olympic edition (Boykoff, 2014), but may stay behind as 'legacies' and extend to other public and urban spaces or contexts.

If we return here to the concept of 'counter-conduct', it is interesting to note that Foucault (2008: 197) observed how this also raised questions such as '[b]y whom do we consent to be directed or conducted? By whom do we want to be conducted? Towards what do we want to be led?'. The contemporary examples described above, both in isolation and when brought together, remain important as they show how some supporters actively resist state and other, non-state actors' attempt to conduct their behaviour and lead fans down towards a path of greater regulation and more invasive surveillance techniques. Governmental techniques and discourses – as seen here through stadium bans, biometric surveillance technologies, legislations – are not passively accepted by all supporters. That is not to say that security and surveillance measures intended to conduct fans are outright *rejected* – or 'the rejection of all forms of conduct', but rather the desire to be conducted 'properly and appropriately' (Foucault, 2008: 231) exist in football fan cultures. Thus, we see traces of Foucault's (1978) insistence that resistance is omnipresent within power regimes. Overall, for Foucault (1978), resistance is always (and has to be) present in regimes of power and, as this section maintains, 'counter-conduct' may help us understand subdued and diffused forms of contemporary fan contestations.

Conclusion

While this chapter is no definite account of fans' resistance towards social control apparatuses in Europe, this chapter produces an argument holding that a culture of resistance and opposition has evolved in parallel with the mechanisms of surveillance and social control that have developed in European football context (both nationally and continentally) since the 1980s, during an epoch of neoliberalism (see also Chapter 2). By describing a number of examples of what we can understand as novel types of 'counter-conduct' among the subjects of football's securitization processes, the fans, this chapter has responded to Spaaij's (2013: 179) suggestion that an 'important [...] avenue for future research can be gleaned from the work of Foucault: the modes of resistance or 'counter-conduct' in the [everyday] practices of football supporters and the issues they coalesce around, especially those used to strategically countervail, weaken or subvert disciplinary matrices'. More specifically, within the notion of 'conduct of conduct', while earlier work displays how football's governing bodies, authorities and the police attempt to 'conduct' fans, this chapter has extended our earlier work by attempting to pay critical attention to how 'counter-conduct' (Foucault, 2008) emerges and may be located within our conceptual, Foucault-inspired model – that is, the 'fan-opticon' (Turner and Lee Ludvigsen, 2023).

This remains important because, according to Foucault (1980: 99), any understanding of 'power' need to recognize its 'infinitesimal mechanisms, which each have their own history, their own trajectory, their own techniques, and tactics', and we might add, temporality. Accordingly, and as this edited collection has demonstrated, academic analyses of 'power' must attempt to avoid the trap of becoming preoccupied with power's centre-point. Through this lens, power is relational. Similarly, we would argue that future sociological and criminological analyses of how football fans are governed and conducted in the twenty-first century also need to account for the extent to which such government is resisted, but also negotiated; how it may be resisted; and how mechanisms of 'counter-power' are *historically* and *temporally* anchored and hence possess their 'own history' and 'own trajectory' (cf. Foucault, 1980).

Notes

1 Important to note, however, not all fans choose to be politically engaged through football, and football fans comprise a diverse social group.
2 The south Wales derby is a fixture between Swansea and Cardiff.

References

Amnesty International (2023) France: Intrusive Olympics surveillance technologies could usher in a dystopian future. *Amnesty International*. Available from: https://www.amnesty.org/en/latest/news/2023/03/france-intrusive-olympics-surveillance-technologies-could-usher-in-a-dystopian-future/ (Accessed: 22 August 2023).

BBC (2019) South Wales football derby: Facial ID technology use criticised by fans. Available from: https://www.bbc.co.uk/news/uk-wales-50142506 (Accessed: 22 August 2023).

BBC (2023) Feyenoord v Roma: No away fans at Europa League quarter-finals. Available from: https://www.bbc.co.uk/sport/football/65183037 (Accessed: 22 August 2023).

Bigo, D (2006) Globalized (in)security: The field and the ban-opticon. In: Bigo, D & Tsoukala, A (eds) *Illiberal Practices of Liberal Regimes: The Insecurity Games*. Abingdon. Routledge, pp. 5–49.

Boykoff, J (2014) *Activism and the Olympics: Dissent at the Games in Vancouver and London*. New Brunswick, NJ. Rutgers University Press.

Carlsson, B & Backman, J (2023) Juridification of fandom: Dealing with spectators' expressions of 'too much joy' in Swedish football. *Soccer & Society* 24(3), 364–377.

Cleland, J, Doidge, M, Millward, P & Widdop, P (2018) *Collective Action and Football Fandom: A Relational Sociological Approach*. Cham. Springer.

De Feijenoorder (2023) Statement: Stop criminalisering voetbalsupporters. Available from: https://defeijenoorder.nl/2023/04/13/statement-stop-criminalisering-voetbalsupporters/ (Accessed: 22 August 2023).

Death, C (2016) Counter-conducts as a mode of resistance: Ways of 'not being like that' in South Africa. *Global Society* 30(2), 201–217.

Della Porta, D (2020) Protests as critical junctures: Some reflections towards a momentous approach to social movements. *Social Movement Studies* 19(5–6), 556–575.

Football Supporters Europe (2022) FSE Calls on EU Parliament to protect citizens from biometric mass surveillance. *FSE*. Available from: https://www.fanseurope.org/news/fse-calls-on-eu-parliament-to-protect-citizens-from-biometric-mass-surveillance/ (Accessed: 22 August 2023).

Foroudi, L (2023) France looks to AI-powered surveillance to secure Olympics. *Reuters*. Available from: https://www.reuters.com/technology/france-looks-ai-powered-surveillance-secure-olympics-2023-03-23/ (Accessed: 22 August 2023).

Foucault, M (1977) *Discipline and Punish: The Birth of the Prison*. Harmondsworth. Penguin.

Foucault, M (1978) *The History of Sexuality. Vol. 1: An Introduction*. New York. Random House.

Foucault, M (1980) *Power/Knowledge: Selected Interviews and Other Writings 1972–1977*. New York. Pantheon.

Foucault, M (2008) *Security, Territory, Population: Lectures at the Collège de France, 1977–78*. Basingstoke. Springer.

Fussey, P & Sandhu, A (2022) Surveillance arbitration in the era of digital policing. *Theoretical Criminology* 26(1), 3–22.

Giulianotti, R (1999) *Football: A Sociology of the Global Game*. Cambridge. Polity Press.

Giulianotti, R (2011) Sport mega events, urban football carnivals and securitised commodification: The case of the English Premier League. *Urban Studies* 48(15), 3293–3310.

Hill, T, Canniford, R & Millward, P (2018) Against modern football: Mobilising protest movements in social media. *Sociology* 52(4), 688–708.

Joern, L (2009) Nothing to hide, nothing to fear? Tackling violence on the terraces. *Sport in Society* 12(10), 1269–1283.

Kossakowski, R, Nosal, P & Wozniak, W (2020) *Politics, Ideology and Football Fandom: The Transformation of Modern Poland*. London. Routledge.

Lee Ludvigsen, J A (2022a) *Sport Mega-Events, Security and Covid-19: Securing the Football World*. London. Routledge.

Lee Ludvigsen, J A (2022b) *Football and Risk: Trends and Perspectives*. London. Routledge.

Lee Ludvigsen, J A (2023a) Football fans' contestations over security: Between offline and online fan spaces and channels. *Sport in Society* 26(10), 1685–1700.

Lee Ludvigsen, J A (2023b) The definers and standard setters of security: Mapping the security field's regulators through European football. *World Leisure Journal* 65(4), 549–566.

May, A (2015) An 'anti-sectarian'act? Examining the importance of national identity to the 'offensive behaviour at football and threatening communications (Scotland) act'. *Sociological Research Online* 20(2), 173–184.

Millward, P (2011) *The Global Football League: Transnational Networks, Social Movements and Sport in the New Media Age.* Basingstoke. Palgrave.

Numerato, D (2018) *Football Fans, Activism and Social Change.* London. Routledge.

Odysseos, L, Death, C & Malmvig, H (2016) Interrogating Michel Foucault's counter-conduct: Theorising the subjects and practices of resistance in global politics. *Global Society* 30(2), 151–156.

Pearson, G (1999) Legitimate targets? The civil liberties of football fans. *Journal of Civil Liberties* 4(1), 28–47.

Pearson, G & Sale, A (2011) 'On the Lash'–revisiting the effectiveness of alcohol controls at football matches. *Policing & Society* 21(2), 150–166.

Pearson, G & Stott, C (2022) *A New Agenda for Football Crowd Management: Reforming Legal and Policing Responses to Risk.* Cham. Palgrave Macmillan.

Rosol, M (2014) On resistance in the post-political city: Conduct and counter-conduct in Vancouver. *Space and Polity* 18(1), 70–84.

Silverstone, D & Lee Ludvigsen, J A (2022) Panic, horror and chaos: What went wrong at the Champions League final – and what needs to be done to make football safer. *The Conversation.* Available from: https://theconversation.com/panic-horror-and-chaos-what-went-wrong-at-the-champions-league-final-and-what-needs-to-be-done-to-make-football-safer-184182.

Spaaij, R (2013) Risk, security and technology: Governing football supporters in the twenty-first century. *Sport in Society* 16(2), 167–183.

Testa, A (2018) The all-seeing eye of state surveillance in the Italian football (soccer) terraces: The case study of the football fan card. *Surveillance and Society* 16(1), 69–83.

The Guardian (2019) Manchester City warned against using facial recognition on fans. *The Guardian.* Available from: https://www.theguardian.com/technology/2019/aug/18/manchester-city-face-calls-to-reconsider-facial-recognition-tech.

Tsoukala, A (2008) *Football Hooliganism in Europe: Security and Civil Liberties in the Balance.* Basingstoke. Palgrave Macmillan.

Tsoukala, A, Pearson, G & Coenen, P (eds) (2016) *Responses to Football 'Hooliganism' in Europe.* The Hague. Springer.

Turner, M (2017) Modern English football fandom and hyperreal, 'safe', 'all-seater' stadia: examining the contemporary football stage. *Soccer & Society* 18(1), 121–131.

Turner, M (2021) 'We are the vocal minority': The Safe Standing movement and breaking down the state in English football. *International Review for the Sociology of Sport* 56(7), 962–980.

Turner, M (2023) *The Safe Standing Movement in Football: Fan Networks, Tactics and Mobilisations.* London. Routledge.

Turner, M & Lee Ludvigsen, J A (2023) Theorizing surveillance and social spacing through football: The fan-opticon and beyond. *Sociology Compass* 17(2), 1–14.

Turner, M & Millward, P (2023) Social Movement Ruptures and Legacies: unpacking the early sedimentation of the anti-European Super League movement in English football. *Sociology*, 1–18, online first.

Index

Note: *Italic* page numbers refer to figures and page numbers followed by "n" denote endnotes.

AB InBev 54, 58
advertisement 51; alcohol sponsorship and 51, 52; campaigns 52
Advisory Group on Tackling Sectarianism in Scotland (AGTS) 67, 70
aesthetic spacing 21, 27, 31, 33
alcohol 11; associations between violence and 53; legalisation of 57; relationships between professional sport and 50–53, 57; and sport industries 50
alcohol commercialisation 56–57; legalisation of 55
alcohol consumption 29, 50, 53, 56–57; legalisation of 53–55; at WC2022 45
alcohol-fuelled supporters 26
alcohol-related sponsors 51
Amara, M 36
American soccer: brand itself in liberal progressive lens 79–80; cultural extraction 80
Amnesty International 106–107
Angel City FC 86–87, 90
ANTIFA 77, 91
anti-fascism 77, 81, 91, 92; politics of 85; queerness and 86
anti-fascist queerness 83–86, *85*
anti-indentarian fan subculture 82–83; anti-fascist queerness 83–86, *85*; diasporic expressions 86–87
'anti-Irish racism' 66, 71
anti-social behaviour 1
antisocial behaviours 15; in Poland 19n1

Arab World Cup 44
Artificial Intelligence surveillance 106
Asian Cup 39, 47
association football 22
Atkinson, M 2
authenticity 22–24
Azevedo, Luiz Carlos 55

Bairner, A 68
Bandura, C 52
ban-opticon 102
Bauman, Z 5, 21–26, 29; *Postmodern Ethics* 24
Bentham, Jeremy 102
Bettine, M 50
Beynon, J 25
Biblioteca Nacional 54
Biernacki, Marek 14
Bigo, D 102
biometric mass surveillance techniques 106
'The Birth of Tragedy' (Nietzsche) 29
Blackshaw, T 2, 22
Borussia Dortmund 27
Bradley, J M 70
Brannagan, P M 40
Brazil: alcohol (see alcohol); daily newspapers in 54; FIFA Men's World Cup (2014) 49–52; local newspaper in 58
Brazil, Russia, India, China, and South Africa (BRICS) 49
Bruce, S 66
Budweiser 54

Callamard, Agnes 107
campaigns 103–104; advertisement 52; Major League Soccer 92; National Women's Soccer League 92; 'Watching Football is not a Crime' 105
Catholicism 65
Catholics, conflict between Protestants and 65, 66
Champions League (2022) 43
civil war, in Northern Ireland 65
Cleland, J 40, 71
club ban 11, 12
cognitive spacing 21, 24, 33; and authenticity 22–24
Collins, T 50
commercialization 19; of football 9, 10; of mass events 10
'common knowledge' 104
communication tools 64
CONCACAF Gold Cup 78, 93
Confederations Cup (2013) 54, 55, 57
Conquergood, D 81
Constitutional Tribunal 11
consumption: alcohol 29, 50, 53, 56–57 (*see also* alcohol consumption); cultural 51–53, 58
contemporary FMEs 39
contested spaces 5, 21–22
Correio Braziliense 54–58
'counter-conduct' 101, 103, 108; football fans and 104–107
'counter-power' 102, 103; resistance/ opposition through ideas of 104
COVID-19 pandemic, NHS personnel during 43
Crabbe, T 2
criminalization: of football fandom 101; of football fans 106; scope of 15; of sectarianism in football 69–71
"critical generosity," notion of 81
cross-disciplinary research agenda 5
crowd management 44
crowd management theories 39
cultural consumption 51–53, 58
cultural extraction 80, 97; MLS and NWSL engage in 87; policing and resistance 90–96; purpose of 81
cultural labor 82, 92
cultural manuals 52
cultural norms 58, 70, 81
cultural shocks 58

Cunha, T 57
Curran, C 71

Decat, Erich 55
definitional power 3
diasporic expressions 86–87
Dionysian pleasures 29–30
disorder 2, 5; *see also* social disorder
dispositifs 3
Dolan, J 81
drinking 29–31
Dróżdż, Mateusz 5
Duffy, Shane 71–72
Dunning, E 27

Eick, V 54
Elias, N 27
emic strategies 23, 24
England, changes in law 10
English football: modernisation of 21, 32; post-1989 modernisation of 23, 33; resistance to modernisation of 25
English Football Association 21
Entman, R 53, 54, 57
Estatuto do Torcedor 54–57
Euro 2012 12, 14
Euro 2020 1, 41, 100
Eurocentric cosmopolitanism 87
European Championships 14
European Convention 11
European football context 103, 107–108
experiential intensity 27–28, 31; standing and pyros 28–29
extractive culture 81, 93; challenges of 96–97

facial recognition technology 46
fan behaviours: evolution of law 14; ineffective fans' resistance 16–18; in Poland 10; relationship between legal tools and 9
fan communities 9, 18; mobilization of resources within 17
fan-consumers support 9
fan cultures 4, 68, 69; contestations in Portland and Los Angeles 80; extraction and commodification 88–90; ideas of authenticity 82; interrelations between police and 38
fan experience 36, 38, 45
fan-generated culture 88, 89

fan groups 82; align with anti-establishment politics 82; resist maneuvers 83
fan-opticon 100–101, 107; extending 101–103
fans' collective identity 17
fan subculture 80, 81; anti-indentarian 82–87; risk of restraining 91
fascism, greyscale against 92, *95*
Fédération Internationale de football association (FIFA) 49, 56, 57, 78
Feyenoord 106
FIFA Club World Cups (FCWC) 40
FIFA Men's World Cup (2014) 49–58
FIFA Men's World Cup (2018) 78
FIFA Men's World Cup (WC2022) 35–37, 39; acquisition of 40; COVID-19 pandemic 41; fan festival and fan village cabin sites at 45; incidents of criminality at 45; international security personnel 43; politics of protest 44
Finn, G 65–66
Flint, J 66
football community, decoding of 22
football fandom 67–69; and 'counter-conduct' 104–107; criminalization of 101, 106
football fanzines movements 104
football hooliganism 2
football mega-events (FMEs) 35–37, 47; media coverage of 38; in Qatar 39–41
football-related crime 18
football-related disorder 2
Football Supporters Association (FSA) 105
football violence 9
Foucault, M 3, 53, 101, 102, 104, 105, 107, 108; *Security, Territory and Population: Lectures at the College de France 1977–1978* 105
frame analysis, legalisation of alcohol consumption 49–59
freedom 29; and drinking 29–31; and novelty 31–32

Gamson, W 53
GCC diplomatic crisis 41
Gee, S 51
gender: non-normative sexualities and 85; and sexuality 83
gender diverse group 91

Ghaill, M M 66
Giulianotti, R 9, 40
Glasgow Celtic FC 67–69, 72, 73
Global North 49, 50
Global South 49, 50, 58
Gloria 85, *85,* 91; Sunday White with 85, *85*
Gorringe et al. (2012) 44
Graeff, B 49–50
Griffin, T R 35
Groombridge, N 2
Gulf Cooperation Council (GCC) 35
Gutierrez, D 50

Hall, S 81
Hamilton-Smith, N 70
hard power 36, 37, *37,* 43
Hayya Card system 42
Hebdige, D 82
hegemonic masculinity group identity 52
Henderson, Chris 6
hermeneutic community 22–23
Heysel tragedy 4
Hillsborough stadium disaster 4, 10, 14
homophobia 79–80, 92; greyscale against 92, *95*
hooliganism *see* stadium hooliganism
hooligans 3, 12, 13, 16, 18, 38
hyper-partisanship manifests 97

identities: construction of 66; Scottish-Protestant identity 68
in-game broadcasting 52
International Alliance for Responsible Drinking Guiding Principles 52
International Centre for Sports Security 42–43
international media 50, 58
International Olympic Committee (IOC) 49
International Paralympic Committee (IPC) 49
International Police Coordination Centre 42
internet 64–65
Ireland, migration from 65
Irish-Catholic-Republicans 65
Iron Front 77, *78, 79,* 85–86; DIY creation of 92; MLS banned 91–93, *92, 94–96*
Ishac, W 36

Jackson, S 52

Kelly, J 66
key spaces, of football 3
Kick it Out 70
Kilvington, D 71
King, S 88
Kossakowski, R 5, 103
Kypri, K 51

Last Mile Security Conference 42
Latino/a/x communities 89, 93–96; diversity of 80
Law on the Safety of Mass Events 10–13, 15, 18
Lech Poznań 13, 19n1
legal tools: evolution of 10; in Poland 15; relationship between fan behaviour and 9
Legia Warsaw 13, 18, 19n1
legislative transformations, analysis of 9
'legitimate targets' 3, 4
Lei Geral da Copa 54–57
Lennon, Neill 69
LGBTQ+ LAFC supporters 94
Liberty 105
'licensed Safe Standing' 100
linguistic errors 15, 18
Lipsitz, G 87
Los Angeles: contestations over fan culture 80; culturally diverse fan base in 93; diasporic expressions 86–87; independent supporter groups in 80; Pride Republic and puto chant 93–96
Los Angeles FC (LAFC) 78, 80, 86–88; and LA Galaxy 89, 96; supporter culture 90; supporter groups of 88–89
Luhmann N 53

MacDougall, D 27
Madison, D S 81
Major League Soccer (MLS) 77, 80, 90, 97; banned Iron Front mark 91–93, *92, 94*–96; campaigns 92; corporate structures of 82; white spatial imaginary of 87–88
"market of generosity" 88
masculinity: conceptualisations of 25; and morality 25–27
mass events: ban on admission to 13; commercialization of 10; law on the safety of 18; organization of 11; prohibition of access to 13; safety of 10
McBride, M 66, 69, 70
McClean, James 72
McGeady, Aiden 72
Messi, Lionel 46
Mexican football 78
Mexican stadium culture 80
Millwall's Old Den stadium 23
Millward, P 2
al-Mohannadi, Hamad Ahmed 46
moral action 24–25
morality 24, 25; masculinity and 25–27
moral spacing 21, 24–25, 33
Muñoz, J E 84

National Union of Supporters' Associations 17
National Women's Soccer League (NWSL) 77, 80, 97; campaigns 92; corporate structures of 82; white spatial imaginary of 87–88
natural attitude 22, 23
Nietzsche, F: 'The Birth of Tragedy' 29
Nil by Mouth 70
Northern Ireland: Catholic-Protestant divide in 64; civil war in 65; conflict in 65
novelty 31–32
Numerato, D 104–105
Nyaupane, Pratik 6
Nye, Joseph 37

O'Brien, K 51
Offensive Behaviour at Football and Threatening Communications (Scotland) Act 2012 (OBFA) 69, 70
Olympic and Paralympic Games 49, 50, 58
online abuse 72, 73
organized fan groups 82
out-of-game broadcasting 52
outsourcing agreements 43

Palmer, C 52
panopticon prison model 102
Pearson, G 3, 44, 101
Peña, E A 81
Penfold, C 71
Petersen-Wagner, R 6, 50

phagic strategies 23, 24
Pinto, Paulo Silva 56
pitch-invasions 1
Pogoń Szczecin 19n1
Poland: antisocial behaviours in 19n1; fan behaviour in 10; law dedicated to football matches in 10–14; legal changes in 15; legal system in 10, 11; stadium hooliganism 10–12; 'war on hooliganism' in 104
Polish Cup 12, 13, 16, 19n1
politicization, of fandom 'issue' 14–16
Portland: anti-fascist queerness 83–86, *85*; contestations over fan culture 80; endorsing Riveters and Timbers Army 81; fan groups 93; greyscale against hand me down blues banner 92, *96*; greyscale against racism, fascism, homophobia banner 92, *95*; independent supporter groups in 80; MLS banned Iron Front mark 91–93, *92*, *94–96*
Portland Thorns FC 77
Portland Timbers FC (PTFC) 77, 86, 88; marketing 88; over-looks performances 89; persists with homoliberal appeals 90; team management of 77
Postmodern Ethics (Bauman) 24
power: 'counter-power' 102, 103; definitional power 3; hard power 36, 37, *37*, 43; smart power 36, *37*, 37–39, *38*; soft power 38, 43, 46
practical attitude 22
Price, J 71
Pride Republic 93–96
principium individuationis 29–30
Procedural Justice Theory 39
professional sport, relationships between alcohol and 50–53, 57
Project Euro 2012 17
Project Stadia 42
protest 103–104
Protestant community 68; conflict between Catholics and 65, 66
Protestantism 65
public disorder, in football 2
public order, threats to 16
Purves, R 52
puto chant 78–80, 93–96
pyrotechnics 28

Qatar 35; football mega-events in 39–41; Hayya Card system 42; infrastructure 35; investment in mega-events 36; investment in sport 35–36; relationship with Iran 44; social control in 37; World Cup Supreme Committee for Delivery and Legacy 41

racism 66, 80, 92; greyscale against 92, *95*
Rangers FC 67–69, 72, 73
regulations: absence of 11; in both 'offline' and 'online' settings 105; in force, United Kingdom 12; of mass event organizer 11; into Polish legal system 10; tightening of 14
regulatory regime 2
Reis, H dos 53, 58n1
religious groups, conflict between 65, 66
resistance 103–104
resistant politics 80–83, 89
Ricoeur, P 26
Riveters 83–86, 88, 90–92; over-looks performances 89
Rookwood, J 6, 40
Rosol, M 105
Rothman, S B 37, 40
Roussef, Dilma 54, 56

'Safe Standing' 100, 102, 103
safety 2; of mass events 10
Sandvoss, C 21
Sassine, Vinicius 55
Scanlon, Christie 6
Scotland: Catholic-Protestant divide in 64; changing societal landscape in 66; emblematic nature of mainstream culture in 68; forms ranging from discrimination, prejudice, and violence 64; sectarianism in 65; sectarian tensions in West 65; sour intricacy of sectarian views in 65; underpinning of sectarianism in 73
Scottish-Protestant identity 68
Seattle Sounders FC 78
sectarian abuse 71–72
sectarian antagonisms 68
sectarianism: criminalization of 69–71; criminal justice system to tackle 73; deficit of academic work on 66; defined as 64, 67; effects on victims 72; and football fandom 67–69;

negative aspect of 64; origins of contemporary forms 65; in Scotland 65; unpacking 65–67
securitisation: correlation between politics, diplomacy and 44; international relations and 37; mechanisms of 41–43
security 2; World Cup operations 41–42
Security and Safety Operations Committee 42
Security, Territory and Population: Lectures at the College de France 1977–1978 (Foucault) 105
Seffrin, F 57
sensate-emotional pleasures 27
singular community 22
situational ethics 26
'skybox' lounges 11
smart power 36; and social control 37, 37–39, *38*
smart stadium initiatives, analysis of 36
"Soccer For All" slogans 89
social control 1, 100; apparatuses of 3; cultural and spatial consequences and social costs of 1; experiences and impacts of 43–46; historical significance of 4; mechanisms 2–3; in Qatar 37; responses 2; smart power and *37*, 37–39, *38*
social control agents 3
social control mechanisms 101; effectiveness of 101
social costs 4
social disorder 1; cultural and spatial consequences and social costs of 1; in football 2; historical significance of 4; incidents of 4
social exclusion 21
social media 64–65; and sectarian abuse 71–72
social media platforms 71, 72
'social problem' 9
social sensitivity 9
social spacing 21, 24
soft disempowerment 37, 38, *38*, 40, 43
soft power 38, 43; acquisition of 38; potential fluidities of 46
sponsorship agreements 35
Sporting Events Act, 1985 28
sport mega-events (SMEs) 36, 37, 46, 49, 50

Sports Crowd Security and Safety Programme 42
sports events: evolution of 11; evolution of law 14
stadium ban procedure 13
stadium hooliganism 15, 16, 32; in Poland 10–12; stadium ban procedure 13
stadium-related criminal activity 15
Stoke City 105
Stott, C 44
Sunday White 92, *93*; with Gloria 85, *85*
supporter behaviour 21, 24
supporter cultures 90
supporter groups 86–88, 95; of LAFC 88–89
surveillance cultures, normalization of 107
surveillance techniques 21

Taylor, D 82
Al-Thani, H 41
Thatcher, Margaret 104
al-Thawadi, Hassan 40
theoretical attitude 22
Thompson, K 52
Timbers Army 83, 85, 88, 91, 92; over-looks performances 89
Tokyo Olympics 41
tragedies 2; Heysel 4; Hillsborough stadium disaster 4, 10, 14
Trump, Donald 92
Tsoukala, A 2, 3, 101
Tusk, Donald 16, 104

UEFA 2023 Champions League 1–2
UEFA Europa League 106
UEFA European Football Championship 10, 12, 16
Ultra groups 68–69
United Kingdom: Irish migrants in 65; laws in 9; migration to America and 66; policies towards football-related offenses 69–70; regulations in force 12; Sporting Events Act, 1985 28; 'war on hooliganism' in 104
US fan-generated culture 82
US professional soccer 77, 87, 97

Valcke, Jerome 57
Vamplew, W 50, 51

vandalism 16
Vargas, V 56
Vendrame, A 52

'war on hooliganism' 104
Watan Exercise 42
'Watching Football is not a Crime' campaign 105
Whigham, S 66
White American fanbase 80
'whitewashing effect' 66

Wittgenstein, L 23
Woolsey, Ian 5–6
World Cup Shield Operation 43
World Cup Supreme Committee for Delivery and Legacy 41

xenophobia 80

Youande Stadium disaster, Cameroon 1
Young, K 2